Thanks to the ever-patient Mr. Bryan, Leah, and Buster.
And to Chamuel and the angels of love.

About the Author

Gwyneth Bryan grew up fifteen minutes from the ocean in southern New Jersey, and currently works in the Princeton, New Jersey, area. She is an intuitive tarot and astrology consultant and teacher, as well as a second level Reiki practitioner.

A lifelong spiritual seeker, Gwyneth was a founding member of the South Jersey Jung Seminar and the Inner Workshop, as well as a long-time member of the Association for Research and Enlightenment (A.R.E.) in Virginia Beach, Virginia. She has participated in numerous workshops there in transpersonal psychology, dream interpretation, intuition studies, reincarnation, and karma, as well as similar workshops at the Orianna Center in Philadelphia and the Center for Relaxation and Healing near Princeton. Gwyneth studied tarot with Djuna Wojton and has worked with astrologer Jacob Schwartz to advance her knowledge in that field.

In her "other life," she is an award-winning arts reporter and critic for a magazine in central New Jersey. Gwyneth has also written for the *Philadelphia Inquirer* and its *Sunday Magazine*, *Prevention*, *New Jersey Life*, the *Newark Star-Ledger*, *New Frontier*, and the magazine of the New Jersey Holistic Association. She has a bachelor's degree in music (minor in philosophy and religion) from Susquehanna University and has studied journalism and creative writing at the University of Pennsylvania as well as Richard Stockton College. She is married to "Mr. Bryan" and lives in a colonial town next to a pocket of green, somewhere off the New Jersey Turnpike. Two ginger tabbies let them live there.

HOUSES

An Astrological Guide

GWYNETH BRYAN

Llewellyn Publications
Woodbury, Minnesota

First Edition
Second Printing, 2010

Cover art by Eric Williams
Cover design by Adrienne Zimiga
Edited by Andrea Neff
Design and format by Donna Burch
Llewellyn is a registered trademark of Llewellyn Worldwide Ltd.

Chart wheels were produced by the Kepler program by permission of Cosmic Patterns Software, Inc. (www.AstroSoftware.com)

Cataloging-in-Publication Data for this title is on file at the Library of Congress.
ISBN-13: 978-0-7387-0868-3
ISBN-10: 0-7387-0868-2

Llewellyn Publications
A Division of Llewellyn Worldwide Ltd.
2143 Wooddale Drive
Woodbury, MN 55125-2989
www.llewellyn.com

Printed in the United States of America

Contents

Charts

Chart data for celebrities came from AstroDatabank (www.astrodatabank.com).

Chart data for anonymous case studies came from client files.

Introduction

If I read another astrology text that tells me to beware of secret enemies, that author might find herself with a surprise foe of her own. I'm from New Jersey—I don't need secret enemies. You get on the turnpike here and there's always some guy in a BMW, speeding, talking on his cell phone, running you off the road while flipping the bird, while a tractor-trailer tailgates you, and that is quite enough intrigue for me, thank you. Maybe that's one good thing about living here. Your enemies are easy to spot.

But I digress. The point is, sometimes we look to astrology for guidance and instead we get perplexed. Sometimes we postmodern gals (and guys) get annoyed by the sheer political incorrectness of the material. Or, a book will obviously predate the feminist movement. One author wrote of "working toward perfecting the feminine trait of submissiveness." Yegads! Didn't submissiveness go out with antimacassars? Try being submissive where I live and you really will get run over.

I stumbled on one text that warned me—with my Mars conjunct Uranus—to "stay out of speeding motorcars and aeroplanes." How very Edwardian! An "aeroplane." Visions of corsets, hobble skirts, and the foxtrot popped into my head.

Mostly, the older books were simply written before the mainstream acceptance of psychology, psychoanalysis, and self-help. All of these are reasons why astrology needs to be brought into the twenty-first century, the age of contemporary psychology, postmodern metaphor, and symbolic, archetypal analysis. The graying generation of astrology books has way too many literal interpretations. For example, do you have a loaded Twelfth House? You're going to jail, pal. Saturn in the Fifth House? Sorry, no children for you.

Just reading some of these things might send people into therapy, or at least provoke unnecessary worrying. I believe planting a negative idea in someone's head also gives the possibility of obsessing until this black cloud of thought becomes a self-fulfilling prophecy. That's where the understanding of symbolism and metaphor comes in.

Go into a bookstore and you'll see a plethora of astrology books—many, many based on solar astrology, and others focused on the Moon, the Ascendant, aspects, even nodes and asteroids. But there are very few books on the houses themselves, at least few good books. Yet the houses—the signs on the cusps, the planets located within—are just as important and have just as much potential effect on a personality.

A new book on the houses, written with pop-culture savvy, intuition, and a bit of humor, can bring the subject into contemporary light. I believe the best use of an astrological chart is as a kind of map to the psyche.

Wouldn't it be great if enlightened parents took their children to a combination astrologer/therapist who could look at the chart and say, "Pay extra special attention to *this* part of your child's personality" or "Cut him a little slack here—he's loaded with air signs" or "Be sure to give her extra love—Pluto is in such-and-such house"? You might be able to anticipate strengths, weaknesses, and lessons to learn. Later on in life, this knowledge might help the grown child choose a vocation, life partner, and friends. That's my prophylactic, or preventive, slant to astrology.

The bottom line is, you should never look at your chart and feel destined for unhappiness. Yes, I believe we are put here on Earth to learn awareness, but also to be happy. Understanding the metaphors, symbolism, and archetypes in our charts—our personal mythology—is a way to understand and forgive ourselves as well as our loved ones and enemies, secret or not so secret. When we can get past our hang-ups, we can work toward cultivating higher consciousness, which benefits everyone.

With *Houses*, I hope to have created a book with updated, contemporary astrological information and analysis. I've blended my astrological studies with my knowledge of psychology and the self-help/self-actualization movement—years of studying and reading everything from Jung and to Dr. Phil. Thanks in part to the latter, people are becoming more open to this information. Those interested in astrology are usually introspective to begin with, so fusing the stars with some "armchair analysis" seems a natural blend.

Although the cosmos and prebirth planning have created a blueprint for our lives, within that structure we make our own mythology. Like bards carrying stories, verse, and songs from the ancients, we carry around, tell, and retell "the story of our life"—things told to us by our parents, grandparents, and extended family.

Sometimes these are concepts that give us strength and pride, such as "talent runs in the family" or "you're good-looking, like your grandmother." On the other hand, some ideas we take from the tribe are outmoded and destructive to our self-esteem, such as "you're no good, just like your father."

We can also think destructive thoughts, engaging in negative self-talk, like, "I'm too dumb/old/ADD to learn all this new technology, so those young kids will always have the edge." However, since the astrological houses hold common themes that are all part of the human condition, knowing the strengths and challenges of the planetary and zodiac placements within the houses will help readers rethink and reprogram such negative self-talk, to throw away the outdated mythology.

For example, some of us who straddle certain generations and socioeconomic groups have heard from elders that "the women in this family must make home and hearth a priority over careers and creativity, and to think otherwise is selfish." We listen silently and nod, but deep inside many of us feel suffocated in the home and long to express a hidden talent or skill, to get "out there" and see how we can shine. Those of us who understand house-based astrology then look to the Tenth House of ambition and image outside the home, and we discover the Sun or another powerful heavenly body there. This points to the need—shaped by the stars—to reframe that tribal thinking and family mythology.

The home and hearth might feel right for other women with other things emphasized in other houses (the Fourth House, for example), but it has never resonated for many of us with a Tenth-House Sun. Our spirit dies a little every day when our creativity and talents are denied.

Discovering such a placement might be the key to gathering the courage to say, "Your priorities are not for me. This is what I need to do to fulfill my soul's purpose."

And so, understanding the houses, planets, and signs—tying all this together—helps change antiquated and obsolete "scripts." We move beyond others' fears and limitations and become the authors of our own lives.

This book is not all about teeth-gnashing introspection, however. I have used numerous personal anecdotes, case histories from the charts of clients and friends, and observations of current events, history, and pop culture to elucidate and expand on specific house information. Throughout the book, you will find charts of famous people in contemporary culture or history—and some of my friends, too—to illustrate my points.

Also, I often try to employ humor, which, I believe, is one of the best ways to get an idea across. For example, chapter 5 opens with a little homage to a favorite routine by George Carlin. In chapter 8, I mention my grandmother's picture of Barry Goldwater on the wall, a clue about her staunch Republicanism. (It didn't have much of an effect on me, I must say.) But perhaps you can relate to that. "Yeah, my grandfather was like Archie Bunker. He had a picture of Barry Goldwater on his wall, too!"

So many things are part of our common experience—pictures on the wall, favorite or disliked foods, music, movies and television, comedy, books and magazines, news and current events, quirky relatives and spouses, things that happen in the workplace or on the road. I hope, by mentioning such details, it conveys my reality to you, resonates for you more, helps us build a bridge. That's why I've told so many personal stories—to bring the various houses to life and to connect.

Mostly, I envisioned this book to further motivate readers who are searching to find greater meaning in their lives. I hope this information helps you embrace your challenges and strengths and create a new, more positive personal mythology.

Note that I frequently recommend bolstering self-exploration with some professional individual counseling. Support groups are also excellent choices for those who favor talking things through casually with other people. Many books that might provide food for thought are suggested in the bibliography.

I present *Houses* to inform and entertain, but also to plant the seeds for your soul's growth.

CHAPTER ONE

In the House: An Explanation of House-Based Astrology

There are numerous ways to navigate an astrological chart, but I believe that thoroughly knowing the signs of the zodiac, as well as the planets (including the Moon and Sun) and, importantly, the houses, will provide an excellent foundation for understanding and analyzing one's own or another person's chart. This is how I work with my astrological clients—I utilize their astrological information and combine it with mainstream counseling techniques and advice to provide them with a little armchair psychology. The astrological data helps me penetrate a sometimes complex personality, or someone undergoing a crisis, and also offer suggestions as to how that person might deal and heal—deal with his or her issues and take the first steps on the path of healing.

Most Americans know a little something about astrology—at least their Sun sign—thanks to the popularity of solar astrology; for example, the daily horoscopes printed in newspapers, magazines, and online. Some folks are starting to also be interested in their Moon sign, as well as their personal, or inner, planets, such as Venus and Mars. That's a good sign (no pun intended).

Getting to know the houses—house-based astrology—helps us put together even more pieces of the personality puzzle.

The planets in the solar system indicate essential kinds of energy, such as the Martian in-your-face personality as opposed to loving Venus or rebellious Uranus. The signs of the zodiac indicate the style in which that energy might be expressed. But the houses point to our issues—universal things in our lives that we have to deal with. Family. Health. School. Taxes. Sex. Death.

Interestingly, even though the "stuff" that is in the houses is pretty much common to everyone, paradoxically it is also very personal, since house-based astrology relies on an individual's time and place of birth. That's what makes house-based astrology in-depth, complex, and distinct.

You may work with a few folks who share your Sun sign, and you might connect on a superficial level. If you were born in the same year, you might also have some of the same planets in the same signs. But it is highly unlikely—unless you were separated at birth!—that you'd be born in the same place and at the same time. That contributes to meaningful differences in the charts that make for more-than-subtle variations between persons with even the closest of Sun signs.

For example, I love to be out at restaurants in late July and most of August to look around and see who is having a grand cake and candles delivered to their table. Those Leo cats and kittens always seem to especially glow when someone sings "Happy Birthday" to them in public. They love to be feted. That's pretty much a given.

But, look more closely. Are they pawing giant prezzies with big gold bows at a table full of noisy friends, or are they gazing into the eyes of a significant other handing over an exquisite bauble? That Leo person's sunny personality could be colored by the position of various planets in the houses. The Sun or other planets could be in the Twelfth House, for example, which makes the personality more subdued—sometimes downright shy. Or the individual could have Saturn in an important personality place in the chart, such as the First House.

To use a musical metaphor, if the elements of solar astrology are the main notes of a melody, then the planetary placements in the various houses are like the harmonies in a song. The houses are like that—they contain the substance that is always there and colors our lives. These are the matters that shape and challenge us and often need to be overcome in order for the soul to grow.

As a believer in karma and reincarnation, I frequently write about how our lives here on Earth, these various incarnations, are like going to school for the soul's growth. Some of us are puttering around in the lower grades, some of us are in high school, and some members of the human race (perhaps those dealing with the most profound and difficult issues) are in college or graduate school. We can look to the houses to see exactly what those issues are, perhaps examine where the karma came from, and, best of all, explore paths to work with it in a positive way.

Before we discuss what exactly that stuff in the houses is, let's try to visualize the wheel of the twelve houses. (We will discuss the importance of the angles in the wheel, as well as the different house systems, later on).

The horoscope wheel is divided by two axes into the Eastern and Western (left and right) hemispheres as well as the upper and lower hemispheres. The wheel or circle is then divided again, like the spokes of a bicycle wheel, into twelve equal sections (in the Equal House system—see chapter 3 for further discussion of the different house systems). Each house represents an area of human life.

The face of a clock is another good way to visualize the houses, except that astrologers want to start at the nine o'clock position, to the left. That is the cusp (edge) of the First House, which lies along the latitudinal line that divides the wheel into an upper and a lower portion. That point indicates the horizon—where the Sun was rising on the astrological clock.

To the far right—the three o'clock position—is the cusp of the Seventh House, or the Descendant. That's where the Sun was setting.

Draw a line from the midnight position of the clock down to six o'clock to divide the horoscope wheel again, vertically, or longitudinally. The top of the wheel is the cusp of the Tenth House, also called the *Medium Coeli* (MC) or Midheaven. That's high noon on your birthday. Directly below is the *Imum Coeli* (IC), the bottom, sometimes called the nadir.

Planets close to the MC are located in the highest possible place in the heavens at the time of birth, whereas planets near the IC are "beneath our feet," on the other side of the Earth. Remember that for practical purposes our wheel is drawn on a piece of paper, so it's flat, but an individual's horoscope embodies three dimensions—we exist on Earth, but the heavens are all around us.

Now that we have an idea of how the chart is divided into houses, we can touch upon general themes connected with each section or house.

First House

The sign at the cusp of the First House tells us about a person's temperament, overall constitution, and persona. It is the natural house for Aries (because Aries is the first sign in the zodiac) and is ruled by Mars. This is the Ascendant (ASC), which, along with the Sun and Moon, is one of the most important factors in analyzing a horoscope. Many astrologers look to the Ascendant to understand the foundation of a person's psyche, what the person draws upon to present himself or herself to the outer world. When I do a chart, I work with the Ascendant to understand the public face rather than the inner self, which is more the territory of the Moon and Saturn. Planets in the First House have considerable power, almost as much as the placement of the Sun in the individual's chart.

Second House

The Second House indicates the material circumstances we are born into, possessions, and also emotions. It is the natural house for Taurus and is ruled by Venus.

Third House

The Third House describes our siblings, early education, immediate environment, and ways of getting around. It is the natural house for Gemini and is ruled by Mercury.

Fourth House

The Fourth House tells us about land, a sense of home and loyalty to one's family, domestic life and parents (especially the mother), and circumstances at the end of life. Ruled by the Moon and associated with Cancer, this is also where we find the *Imum Coeli* (IC). Like the ground beneath our feet, the IC represents where we might like to "plant" ourselves, how we were nurtured by our family of origin, and the ancestral and karmic influences that color our lives. Look to the Fourth House for deep psychological issues, "buried treasure," and matters of the unconscious. There is a lengthier discussion of the IC in chapter 2.

Fifth House

The Fifth House indicates creativity, play, exploring the arts, that first flame of romance, children, and games of risk. This is the natural house of Leo and the Sun.

Sixth House

The Sixth House tells us about work, work, work, and also diet, health, exercise, hobbies, and our attitudes toward subordinates. Mercury rules this house, which is associated with Virgo.

Seventh House

The Seventh House is the domain of learning to cope with partnerships and mature relationships, such as marriage and business relationships. It is the house of Libra and Venus. It is also where the Descendant is located.

Eighth House

The Eighth House delves into more complex issues such as grasping human mortality, sexuality, and the mysteries of life and death. This house also has to do with "other people's money" and communal goods such as investments and taxes. It is ruled by Pluto and is the natural house of Scorpio.

Ninth House

The Ninth House governs higher education, religion, philosophy, and getting to know what other cultures believe and then comparing those beliefs with our own. It is ruled by Jupiter and associated with Sagittarius.

Tenth House

The Tenth House describes our occupations, achievements in the outer world, ambitions, and aspirations. This is the natural house of Capricorn, ruled by Saturn, and is the location of the *Medium Coeli* (MC).

Eleventh House

The Eleventh House tells us about our friends, the community at large, our relationship to humanity as a whole, and our social consciousness. It is ruled by Uranus and connected with Aquarius.

Twelfth House

The Twelfth House is the domain of the metaphysical, which means "beyond" (meta) the physical, personal, or mortal. This house has to do with questions about what might come after we leave the Earth plane and what the soul's "lesson plan" has been. It is also linked to hospitals, monasteries, penitentiaries, and other places of seclusion. The Twelfth House is governed by Neptune and is the natural house of Pisces. Interestingly, with the Twelfth House, the horoscope wheel comes full circle. Reincarnationists believe that planets here also indicate what kind of prebirth planning took place with the soul's higher, etheric guides.

That's a thumbnail sketch of each of the twelve houses. In the chapters on the houses themselves, I will flesh out this information, as well as explain the significance of the planets placed in the houses.

CHAPTER TWO

What's the Angle?
A Special Discussion of the
Imum Coeli and the Descendant

Someday, maybe we'll be able to turn on the holograph machine, as they do in *Star Trek: The Next Generation,* where Captain Picard likes to go to virtual "Paris" in the Belle Epoque. We could place ourselves or our clients at the center of a three-dimensional virtual horoscope, with the horizon to our left for the First House/Ascendant; the constellations above our heads for the Tenth House/Midheaven and beneath our feet for the Fourth House/*Imum Coeli;* and the virtual, imaginary sunset to our right for the Seventh House/Descendant. Perhaps it will happen in our lifetime.

For now, though, the charts we make as astrologers are one-dimensional and flat, because they're printed on a piece of paper.

We have to use our imagination to think in terms of the "angular" sections of the horoscope wheel. When we first dissect the circle that makes up the wheel with horizontal and vertical lines, the "angular" houses are where those lines intersect with the outer edge of the circle—the cardinal points of the wheel.

More importantly, we need to know what the dynamics of these entities (the IC, MC, Ascendant, and Descendant) and their corresponding houses mean.

Much has been written about the First House/Ascendant and the Tenth House/MC, including extended discussion in the later chapters on these particular houses. In this section, however, I would like to say a few things about the less understood cusps of the Fourth and Seventh Houses—the *Imum Coeli* (IC) and Descendant, respectively.

The *Imum Coeli*/Cusp of the Fourth House of Roots

Like the ground beneath our feet, the IC represents where we might like to "plant" ourselves, how we were nurtured by our family of origin (in this incarnation), and the ancestral and karmic influences that color our lives. I also look to the Fourth House for deep psychological issues, matters of the unconscious, and what authors and therapists Lindsay River and Sally Gillespie called "buried treasure" in their 1987 book *The Knot of Time*.[1]

Some of these matters and issues have to do with our relationships with our mothers. The Fourth House is ruled by the feminine Moon, a strong indication in a chart of ties to the mother. The sign on the Fourth-House cusp indicates how a child *experiences* his or her mother, not so much what the mother's actual personality is like.

For example, if Jupiter is in the Fourth House, or the sign on the Fourth-House cusp is Sagittarius, the mother may applaud the child if he or she has an outgoing personality, like the typical Archer, and Sagittarian-type interests, such as foreign languages, foreign foods, travel, the outdoors, and sports.

But woe to the child who is a homebody, reserved, and bookish. The mother may prod such a child to be different, to go against the grain of his or her true personality, or will appear disappointed when the child dampens Mama's buzz with introspection. Bummer, man. Children are very sensitive, and it's especially hard when they get the feeling Mom is disappointed—or *just doesn't like them.*

Fortunately, the Fourth House is also the place of buried treasure. Where might the aforementioned serious child go to find "gravitas"? If Mom is rocking and rolling and teaching aerobics and flying to Paris, it won't be at home.

It's painful, but sometimes this very lack of connection stimulates such children to dig and find their own interests and strengths.

River and Gillespie explain the treasures of the Fourth House/*Imum Coeli* superbly: "(It) shows an area in the chart which may be prospected for 'buried treasure.' For instance, someone with Uranus in the Fourth House may have had a disrupted family life, or a parent who seemed like an outcast from society, which caused the child much suffering. Buried in the unconscious is the person's own Uranus, her ability to be inventive, brilliantly eccentric, an inspired outsider to the conventional viewpoint."[2]

The authors go on to say that if the proper nurturing isn't present, the IC, on the cusp of the Fourth House, urges us to nurture ourselves, perhaps through psychotherapy, meditation, or creative pursuits.

A fine example of someone who has successfully dealt with challenges of the Fourth House is Gloria Steinem, who has a stellium (group) of planets in the Fourth House, including Saturn. She truly had a troubled childhood and even before her teen years was saddled with the responsibility of taking care of her severely depressed mother after her father abandoned the family. Saturn in the Fourth House can bring a sense of seriousness into the childhood home, and may even reverse the roles of parent and child.

Even with all this responsibility and although she had received a sporadic education in early childhood, Steinem found her own buried treasure. She nurtured herself with books, reading everything she could get her hands on. Witnessing the devastating effects an uncaring husband had on her mother and living through the shock of a splintered family motivated her to explore avenues other than the traditional woman's roles of wife and mother. This planted the seeds to urge other women to reach their personal potential outside the home, which Steinem encouraged through her leadership role in *Ms.* magazine.[3]

Steinem also has a couple planets in the Fifth House, which makes her creative and courageous. She rose from a little girl living in a trailer with a sick mother to a cultural icon of the sixties and seventies—and a role model for other women trapped in unhealthy, dead-end situations. That's the kind of treasure that can be discovered within the depths of the IC and Fourth House.

The fact that the IC is located at the bottom of a chart struck a metaphorical connection with me. In an interview for an arts story I wrote about Brooklyn-based artist Mark di Vincenzo, we talked about the Buddhist philosophy of making "medicine out of poison." He paints mostly watery scenes and is fascinated with the beauty on the surface of a pond as well as the not-so-pretty stuff at the bottom. Indeed, the muck and mud might be lovely

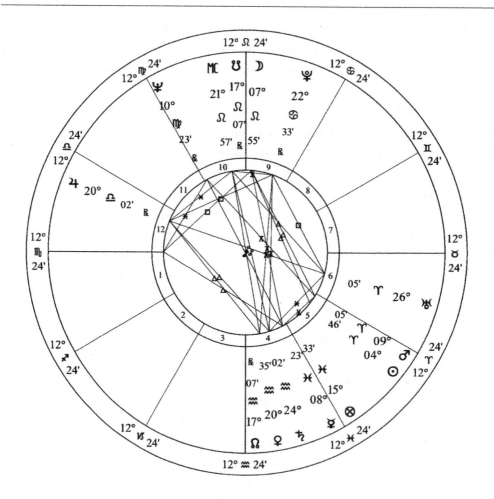

Gloria Steinem
March 25, 1934 / 10:00 p.m. Standard Time
Time Zone: 5 hours West
Toledo, OH / Equal Houses

only to a catfish. But this slimy, decaying matter feeds the lovely water flowers that grow and blossom on the surface—lilies, hyacinths, and lotuses. Mark talked about how he believes we can take the "garbage" in our own lives, and through it, grow as beautifully as the lotus.

That's the essence of the *Imum Coeli*. The cusp of the Fourth House might be considered the "compost pile" of the horoscope—a not-so-pretty place sometimes, but one from which great growth is possible.

The Descendant/Cusp of the Seventh House of Partnership

Moon and Sun. Yin and yang. Masculine and feminine. Light and shadow.

Perhaps this last concept is the best one to use to foster an understanding of the Descendant, which lies on the cusp of the Seventh House of partnership.

If the Ascendant is where the Sun is rising at the time of one's birth, the Descendant is just the opposite—it's the time and place of the setting Sun. We've basked in the bright luminosity of day, and now the light is changing as the Sun drops below the horizon and disappears, allowing the night and the Moon to share their own splendor.

Photographers often love to make pictures around this time, to capture the colors that accompany sunsets, but also because the low light is sumptuous and rich, and the shadows long and fascinating.

It's the metaphor of the shadow—which characterizes the Descendant. Here, across from the Ascendant, is where we meet the undeveloped, or "shadow," self.

The Ascendant is what we use to put ourselves out there in the real world, an ego-driven persona that helps us make our way.

On the other hand, the Descendant has to do with personality traits that we often have suppressed and sometimes only discover when we meet someone else who reminds us of these traits, disguised or hidden by the ego.

It's the "yin" to one's "yang"—the very behaviors that either repel or attract us. For better or worse, these are shadowy issues in the psyche that have been covered up and need to be exposed to the light.

For example, someone with Leo rising has Aquarius as the Descendant, on the cusp of the Seventh House. Passionate, theatrical, emotional Leo rising can't quite understand cool, logical Aquarius rising, and either dislikes him or her immediately—perhaps dismissing Aquarius as distant, robotic, not interested in l'amour—or else falls in love with the unflappable Water Bearer. And vice versa.

Since the Seventh House is the house of partnerships, where people learn how to negotiate close relationships, this is often where issues of unconscious attraction (or repulsion) are played out. But this is a simple illustration of the "light and shadow" I talk about when contrasting the Ascendant and Descendant.

Using Leo rising again, perhaps when the Lioness meets and misunderstands Aquarius rising, it's because she needs a bit of the Water Bearer's Spock-like logic to counterbalance her emotions and theatrics. On the other hand, Aquarius rising might need to be warmer and more playful.

If you understand the basic attributes of the various zodiac signs on the Ascendant, then you can also easily conceive of their opposites on the Descendant. Organized, hardworking Virgo rising is driven to distraction by numinous, sometimes-needy Pisces rising. "Me first" Aries rising can't understand the "let's be fair and include everyone" philosophy of Libra rising. The Sagittarius Ascendant plans a month-long trip to the other side of the world, immersed in a foreign culture, while Gemini rising wants to take a short jaunt or putter around the neighborhood collecting and sharing gossip, trading quips around the cracker barrel.

Interestingly, the very characteristics in the Descendant that we don't exercise or show to the public—things that often disgust us when we see them in other people—are just the traits we need to develop more in order to become more fully individuated. Sometimes we have deliberately discarded them because we abhor them (at least we think we do), or else we have suppressed them in this incarnation due to karmic factors.

When we are attracted to someone with traits of our Descendant, it's because we're projecting a positive part of our psyche that hasn't been developed yet.

Sometimes psychologists call this falling in love with elements of our personality that we need to strengthen in ourselves.

Conversely, when we find ourselves repelled, we are disgusted because we unconsciously recognize negative, hidden parts of ourselves—the shadow self.

"The disowned part often reappears to haunt us, and we keep meeting people with this strong sign in their charts," write River and Gillespie in *The Knot of Time*.[4] "The disowned self can manifest as a recurrent rival or enemy, turning up in every workplace, every group joined, with a new name and face but sharing the same characteristics."

Another way to think about the gifts of the Descendant is to consider what Edgar Cayce, also known as the Sleeping Prophet, had to say about "meeting self" as part of the soul's development.[5] Thinking in terms of reincarnation, we are actually "meeting" someone who is much like we were in a previous life. This may be a negative trait we needed to grow out of, and now we need to forgive others for having their own issues, knowing that we went through the same thing ourselves—and people forgave and loved us anyway. Or, it could be a gift of the soul that we have forgotten. Rediscovering this trait could change our lives and our relationships for the better.

Either way, understanding the bountiful lessons the Descendant can teach us is like making a work of visual art—photography or painting. Both require shadows and light in order to be fully realized. The human psyche is very much the same. If the Ascendant is the luminosity, then the Descendant is the contrast, the shading.

1. Lindsay River and Sally Gillespie, *The Knot of Time* (New York: Harper & Row, 1987).

2. Ibid., p. 230.

3. *Lois Rodden's AstroDatabank*, "Newsmaker's Chart for Gloria Steinem," http://www.astrodatabank.com/NM/SteinemGloriaPRT.htm.

4. River and Gillespie, p. 236.

5. Kevin Todeschi, *Soul Development: Edgar Cayce's Approach for a New World* (Virginia Beach, VA: A.R.E. Press, 2003).

CHAPTER THREE

House Systems:
A Guide for the Confused

I haven't held a protractor in my hand since freshman year in high school, when I took geometry, and that was a long time ago. That's why computers and computer services to calculate charts have been such a bonus to me and countless other astrologers who sometimes have to squeeze in their practices between the demands of the non-astrology world.

Computerized delineation of the houses by the Equal House system, which is what I use, has also freed me from various mathematical exercises in futility and allowed me to focus on the psychodynamics of the individual whose chart I'm doing.

It's interesting to note that early astrologers worked for upper-class and even royal families and were respected for their knowledge of the configurations of the heavens as well how the movements of the heavenly bodies might portend future events. Astronomy may have even been considered a hobby until astrology and alchemy fell from favor in lieu of the more empirical sciences.[1] However, considering all the geometrical computations astrologers had to make simply to cast a single chart, even a present-day mathematician or engineer should have great respect for these individuals.

I can just envision a robed man of the Renaissance (because court astrologers were most likely men) in a room hung with hand-drawn maps of the stars and a primitive telescope, lit by candlelight, poring over the chart of someone born in Northern lands. The creases on the astrologer's forehead would deepen as he tried to delineate the erratic houses.

That's one of the reasons astrologers were trying to improve on early house systems—the houses were hard to figure in extreme latitudes.

One thing is for certain. House systems can stir controversy among astrologers, especially between those who use charts as a blueprint to understand the individual's personality and those who look more for transits that will color the individual's future.

For some, it's a way to launch a good argument. In her book *Secrets from a Stargazer's Notebook*, Debbi Kempton-Smith writes that she's witnessed astrologers come to blows over which house system is "the best."[2]

Can't you just see angry astrologers threatening each other with, "Let's step outside and settle this metaphysician to metaphysician!"

I'm more interested in looking at the chart and getting to work on the person. The flak over various house systems is kind of like arguing over which incarnation of *Law & Order* is the best: *Criminal Intent, Special Victims Unit*, or the original? They're all good. What is important are the characters and the stories—same with the information that can be gleaned from an individual's chart.

However, since the controversy is out there, and knowledge is power, it's a good idea to discuss the various house systems. I will present the most common systems and then suggest several Web sites and publications for those who are interested in further study.

I mostly use the Equal House system (invented by Ptolemy), where the house cusps are all spaced thirty degrees apart. Once you know a person's birth time and place and can figure the Ascendant, the houses will follow in order around the wheel. The downside to this is that the *Medium Coeli* will usually not correspond with the cusp of the Tenth House.

"Grant Lewi used the Equal house system," writes astrologer and author Jeff Jawer, in an article on house systems on *StarIQ*, the Web site he cofounded.[3] "Some twentieth-century English astrologers promoted it because it did away with the great extremes of house sizes at latitudes far from the equator. It's also found in many traditional systems."

I believe the Equal House system is especially valid for New Age astrologers, who wish to gain knowledge of their clients' psychological and karmic issues and help them work toward their souls' destination.

There is a succinct explanation of some of the other popular house systems on the Web site *Elysian Astrology & New Age Shop*, which explains that the Campanus system was invented by Johannes Campanus, a chaplain and mathematician to the thirteenth-century Pope Urban IV.[4] Campanus was the first to see the significance of using four angles as cusps of the First, Fourth, Seventh, and Tenth Houses. He divided the house wheel at four cardinal points—the Meridian going through the east and west points of the horizon, and the Prime Vertical going through the north and south points. This system produces the most irregularly sized cusps. This phenomenon occurs when drawing a chart for someone born in a far northern latitude.

There also is the Regiomontanus system, devised by astronomer Johannes Müller (1436–76), supposedly to improve on the Campanus system. *Elysian Astrology* says: "This system [Regiomontanus] uses the Equator and the horizon as the two planes cutting the sphere . . . conceptually, the individual is contained within an environment linked to the Earth's movement around the Sun. Regiomontanus is more commonly used in Europe, and might have been more appropriate in a time when people lived in the same place all their lives, for whom the links between the Earth and the Sun are the most important in the horoscope."[5]

The Placidus House system, however, is the most popular in the Western world, according to both Jawer and Kempton-Smith. This is thanks to its accuracy and to the widespread publication and distribution of its tables, especially when astrology became fashionable in Victorian England.

It is named after Italian monk and mathematician Placidus de Tito (1590–1668), who devised a system dividing the time it takes the Ascendant to reach the *Medium Coeli*. Placidus is an unequal house system, often with very large or very small houses for individuals living in northernmost latitudes.[6]

The Koch House system was first presented in 1964 by German astrologer Dr. Walter Koch (1895–1970), a survivor of the Dachau concentration camp, according to Kempton-Smith.[7] Sometimes called the Birth Place Method, this unequal house system uses the notion of a plane of time sweeping down from the *Medium Coeli* to the Ascendant, and is more closely linked to the horizon. The MC is therefore considered the most important point, along with the local geographical environment. The MC here is linked to ego, to who we are and to what we want to become.[8] So, the Koch system emphasizes individual choice and free will and thus became very popular throughout the sixties, seventies, and eighties, with the rise of the self-help and self-actualization movements. Kempton-Smith says it works very well for her in looking at future events and transits, but less so in analyzing a personality.[9]

Other house systems include the time-based Alcabitus (the standard house system in the late Middle Ages), Earth House, Horizontal, Midheaven, Meridian (also called Vehlow-Equal or Zariel), Moon, Morinus, Natural Graduation, Natural Hours, Octopos, Polich-Page (also called Topocentric), Solar, and Sun. The Porphyry system is named for Porphyry (232–304), a Greek philosopher and student of Plotinus. This system seems to be preferred by those who do Vedic, or Jyotish (Indian), astrology.[10]

To learn more about house systems, there are numerous online sites that will provide tidbits or volumes of detailed information. Listed below are just a handful. Or, you can go to a major search engine like Google and type in "astrological house systems" or similar terms.

- http://www.geocities.com/astrologyhouses/housesystems.htm, "Development of House Systems in Astrology after Classical Astrology," by Dr. Shepherd Simpson.

- http://www.aquamoonlight.co.uk/systems.html, "House Systems Used in Astrology," *Aquamoonlight Astrology.*

- http://www.widgetsworld.co.uk/free/astrological.php, *Widget's Astrology World & Company.*

- http://www.elysian.co.uk/astrologyhousesystems.htm, "Astro House Systems," by the Elysian Group, *Elysian Astrology & New Age Shop.*

1. The Elysian Group, "Astro House Systems," *Elysian Astrology & New Age Shop,* http://www.elysian.co.uk/astrologyhousesystems.htm.

2. Debbi Kempton-Smith, *Secrets from a Stargazer's Notebook* (New York: Topquark Press, 1999).

3. Jeff Jawer, "House Cusps and Systems," *StarIQ,* http://www.stariq.com/Main/Articles/P0001054.HTM.

4. The Elysian Group, http://www.elysian.co.uk/astrologyhousesystems.htm.

5. Ibid.

6. Anne Mogul, *Sky View Zone*, http://www.skyviewzone.com/houseinfopop.htm.

7. Kempton-Smith, p. 5.

8. The Elysian Group, http://www.elysian.co.uk/astrologyhousesystems.htm.

9. Kempton-Smith, p. 6.

10. Dr. Shepherd Simpson, "Development of House Systems in Astrology after Classical Astrology," http://www.geocities.com/astrologyhouses/housesystems.htm.

CHAPTER FOUR

First House: The Mirror

If the arrangement of houses was like a Monopoly game board, then the First House would be "Go." This is where it all starts. We roll the dice and see where we land and how we play the game—whether we end up with luxury hotels on Boardwalk and Park Place or a decrepit abode on Baltic.

The First House is associated with birth and very early childhood, personality, and ego. The Ascendant colors and describes one's persona—the character traits we show to the outside world. If a person's Sun sign flavors him with a certain essence or style, and the Moon indicates deeper longings in the individual, the Ascendant or a stellium of planets in the First House shows the outward character traits, how the person presents himself.

The First House also has to do with the physical body—the anatomical shell in which the soul and spirit have been placed. In her excellent book *Astrology and Your Health*, Jeanne Avery puts the First House and the Ascendant into an interesting perspective, likening the Ascendant to a car.

"Imagine driving alone in a foreign land," she writes. "The first choice about the trip is what kind of an automobile will be best suited for the journey. You could choose a Rolls-Royce, a Mercedes or a Ferrari. You may decide to drive a Honda or Toyota.

"The First House describes the structure of the physical body and body language. It tells the story of a person's entry into the world and everything connected with the beginning of his life. The physical body is the protective shell to house the inner self. It shields the soul and spirit from any real or imagined dangers on the earth plane."[1]

So the sign on the cusp of the First House, or Ascendant, indicates what kind of "container" our soul and spirit will be carried around in. Is it a fine Quezal vase (Venus in the First House, perhaps) or a galvanized tub (Mars)? The vase is beautiful, exquisite, singular, but you wouldn't want to have one around if you had boisterous children or curious cats. On the other hand, the galvanized tub isn't pretty at all, but it's very useful. It's something that gets handed down through the generations. People use these tubs for gardening now, but that's where folks used to take their Saturday night baths—sometimes the whole family in the same batch of water on a single night!

My "container," or Ascendant, is Virgo, and although I don't feel smallish, I'm frequently described as petite. My Mercurial First House simply does not make me a big, strong person—which definitely put me at a disadvantage with bullies. Attention to diet has kept my weight down. Nerves and nervous energy whittle it down too. Students of reincarnation and past lives understand that the soul "chooses" its circumstances in each successive life in order to get the best education it can on the Earth plane. I used to scratch my head, wondering why I would "choose" to be a little person when physical strength was admired in my family.

Then, in a past-life regression, I got to "see" why I had made that choice. I was literally a slob in a previous life and could, under trance, see myself lying around, not exercising, eating the wrong foods, looking slovenly, and moving ungracefully. When I was regressed back to the time of death, I saw that I had died of heart disease, brought on by a poor diet. I hovered over that much-larger container, thinking, "I wish I'd taken better care of myself." And so, in this lifetime, I have a small frame and a passionate interest in health.

My husband, with Capricorn as the sign on the cusp of the First House, has a stronger structure, a downright handsome physical frame, because Capricorn, ruled by Saturn, has to do with the skeleton and bone structure. I'll bet many fashion models have Saturn or

Capricorn related to the First House. Designers look for a beautiful skeleton (literally, in the case of Twiggy or Kate Moss) on which to hang their creations.

My husband—a Capricorn-rising realist—would dispute that he's a good-looking Goat, but that's the first thing I noticed: his long legs and arms, high cheekbones—a beautiful skeleton.

Mr. Bryan seems to get better looking as he gets older, too, a trait of Capricorn on the First-House cusp. Fortunately, he doesn't have any challenging aspects to his Ascendant; otherwise that skeleton also might give him problems such as arthritis.

In addition to physical attributes, the First House shows our persona—what kind of character we are playing as we act our way through this great stage play called life. It also colors our tastes and mannerisms. With quixotic Mercury ruling my Ascendant, I'm naturally kind of wired and perfectionistic, like Felix Ungar, the fussy character in *The Odd Couple*. I relate to Felix's need to run that vacuum cleaner and drive Oscar Madison crazy. In fact, I once roomed with a woman sportswriter who wouldn't cap the toothpaste, clean the litter box, or even use plates sometimes. One friend dubbed us "Felix and Oscar."

Mercury (Virgo and Gemini) here, then, makes the native fastidious and nervous, with a facility for mental activity and a way with words and the vacuum cleaner. We Virgo-rising people and First-House Mercuries are good copy editors, and you can find us at the health food restaurant, doing the crossword puzzle.

As for Capricorn rising, such as my husband, the Goat loves things associated with fossils, archaeology, history, and work. Curmudgeonly Capricorn, associated with Saturn, gives these people a certain gruffness, but they're also steadfast and direct.

Planets in this position make a person "pop." They give the individual a lot of charisma that you can't miss. When I looked at Bill Clinton's chart, I was fascinated to see a stellium of planets in the First House. (George W. Bush and Arnold Schwarzenegger also have powerful First Houses.) Venus, Mars, and Jupiter are all there.

First of all, the conjunction or near-conjunction of all these planets is powerful in itself. Venus in the First House gives abundant charm and outstanding artistic ability. Mars makes for a goal-oriented person of action. Jupiter gives optimism, luck, and loquaciousness. That's Clinton all right—he's famous for his riveting and sometimes lengthy speeches, such as the one at the 2004 Democratic Convention. *My Life*, his autobiography, came in

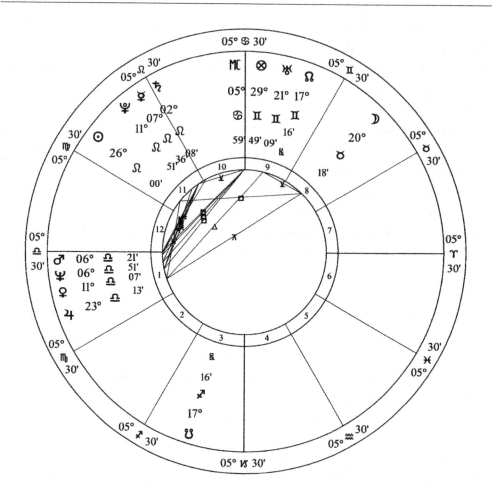

Bill Clinton
August 19, 1946 / 8:51 a.m. Standard Time
Time Zone: 6 hours West
Hope, AR / Equal Houses

at 999 pages, and it takes Clinton almost 500 pages just to get to his days in the White House.

That's Jupiter in the First House—he loves to communicate, and he's so darn good at it. That Jupiterian luck might have contributed to his reputation for coming through various crises intact, which earned him the nickname of "Slick Willie" to his detractors.

And Jupiter here can make for problems with weight. Who can forget those comedy skits about the forty-second president's love for junk food and battle with the scales?

Venus and Mars in Libra on the First-House cusp give him undeniable charm. He was received and applauded like a rock star at the 2004 Democratic Convention—people wanted to nominate him for president again. When he was on his book tour in the summer of 2004, fans camped out for fifteen hours near a bookstore in Mercer County, New Jersey, awaiting Clinton's appearance.

He gets that kind of reception wherever he goes.

On the negative side, Venus in the First House can make a person like pleasure too much, and Jupiter can also indicate a tendency toward self-indulgence. When Clinton was in office, he and his administration did many great things. The economy was good, the deficit was balanced, and there was a feeling of optimism in the country. But what will William Jefferson Clinton be most remembered for? His weakness for the ladies, particularly a beret-wearing intern.

Oh well. It's common knowledge that politicians and other people in the public eye—rock, movie, and sports stars—become famous because of their powerful personalities and charisma. And power is sexually magnetic. Women have always been on the scene in Washington, even hanging on George Washington himself, probably.

But with Clinton, perhaps the various planetary placements in the First House clouded his thinking, or he felt that luck would carry him as it had always done. I like to focus more on his journey from childhood in a broken family to the Oval Office, however. How does a chubby band nerd get to be president of the United States?

A group of well-aspected planets in the First House just might help.

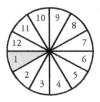 ***First House:*** The natural house of Aries and ruled by Mars, the First House has to do with a person's birth and very early childhood, ego, body type, personality, and outward persona.

Planets in the First House

Sun in the First House

There's a powerful desire to develop a better approach to life or to be in a position of dominance. These individuals are confident, independent, and responsible, but must watch the tendency to be power-seeking or dictatorial. If the Sun has challenging aspects, the person's health may suffer. If the Sun is harmoniously aspected, the individual usually has good health.

Moon in the First House

These individuals are extremely sensitive to their environment. They are restless and impulsive. People with a First-House Moon might wish their lives were different, but they lack the courage to make it so. They must learn to take the emphasis off their emotions, and become genuinely sympathetic and responsive to the needs of others. They are influenced by their early lives, especially the mother, which forms the foundation for their adult approach to life.

Mercury in the First House

These folks are adaptable, inquisitive, eloquent, and humorous. Jacks-of-all-trades, they want to know something about a lot of things. These are the columnists, critics, and pundits of the zodiac, since their speeches and writing reflect their own personal opinions. Jittery nerves help keep these people slender, but could cause long-term, serious health problems.

Venus in the First House

This placement makes these people friendly, magnetic, and usually quite attractive. There is an appreciation for beauty and beautiful things, but also a tendency toward selfishness. This position brings benefits to these individuals—they have the ability to get what they want from life.

Mars in the First House

This placement would be like having Aries on the First-House cusp, since Mars is the Ram's ruling planet. These people have Arien propensities, including abundant physical energy, assertiveness, independence, and also the impulsiveness and impatience the Ram is known for. Those with a First-House Mars have good organizational abilities and lots of self-confidence. They need to use caution and consciously try to slow down, because impulsiveness and speed of movement could make them prone to accidents.

Jupiter in the First House

This First House is a great place for this planet, which makes these natives generous, optimistic, cheerful, and confident, with a lot of energy. They have a love and talent for sports. A First-House Jupiter brings opportunities for personal growth, but also a tendency toward weight problems, since Jupiter is known for its expansiveness. These people have the confidence to become leaders, because they have the ability to inspire faith in others. On the other hand, they can be gullible, egotistical, or self-indulgent.

Saturn in the First House

Saturn in the First House indicates a thorough, penetrating mind, with an ability to get to the heart of the matter. Others may be put off by these people's terseness and tendency to be domineering, pessimistic, or overly serious—they need to lighten up! Folks with this placement present themselves as conservative in appearance and mannerisms—the stiffness is hiding feelings of awkwardness and shyness. On the positive side, these people are unbiased and not prone to favoritism. They can be critical, although it's on an equal-opportunity basis. It may seem like a contradiction, but those with a First-House Saturn have an unbiased quality about criticism. Anyone could be the target of their judgment, not just an enemy. People with Saturn in the First House or on the Ascendant like to maintain a certain amount of personal space and are not inclined toward chumminess. They like to be in control. They are cool cats, but they need self-awareness and perhaps psychotherapy, or they could become downright cold.

Uranus in the First House

Zap! Here's the rebel with a cause. These folks are strong-willed, independent, freedom-loving, and intuitive. They could also be willful or high-strung. They may feel like outsiders—knowing they are different could bring loneliness. They are always blazing trails and seeking new ways to express old ideas. A First-House Uranus makes the intuition strong, and these people would be encouraged to listen to it. They could look a little slovenly, paying little attention to their physical appearance since so much is going on in the mind.

Neptune in the First House

These are the true artists and visionaries of the zodiac. Creativity just seems to flow through their hands organically. They are very tender souls, looking for perfection on Earth, often losing themselves in fantasy. Because they love to escape, they may overdo it with various mind-altering substances or even sweets. Channeling their creative and visionary talent and using it to help others in a very high calling for those with a First-House Neptune.

Pluto in the First House

These folks are courageous, magnetic, self-sufficient, and strong-willed. They have great potential but, sadly, often lack confidence in themselves. They are paradoxically gentle but also skeptical, inconsiderate, and obstinate. They also can be angered easily. This is the position of the loner, the mystery man or woman, difficult to understand. A First-House Pluto brings tremendous healing abilities, both of others and themselves. This position indicates a karmic need to transform their approach to life. They are on Earth to learn to dissolve the residue of obsolete personality traits. They must learn to get over hurts, because brooding will have a negative effect on the physical body.

---

1. Jeanne Avery, *Astrology and Your Health* (New York: Fireside Books, 1991).

CHAPTER FIVE

Second House:
Home and Garden

"Actually this is just a place for my stuff, ya know? That's all, a little place for my stuff. That's all I want, that's all you need in life, is a little place for your stuff, ya know? I can see it on your table, everybody's got a little place for their stuff. This is my stuff, that's your stuff, that'll be his stuff over there. That's all your house is: a place to keep your stuff. If you didn't have so much stuff, you wouldn't need a house. You could just walk around all the time. A house is just a pile of stuff with a cover on it . . . That's what your house is, a place to keep your stuff while you go out and get . . . more stuff!"

—George Carlin, *A Place for My Stuff*[1]

God bless George Carlin. He goes on and on in that 1981 routine about "stuff." And that kind of sums up the Second House—it's a place for stuff.

That is, material things, possessions, property, and money. Think of that Monopoly board again. The First House is "Go," and now the dice have been rolled and we're in the game, moving around the board or the wheel of houses. Perhaps you've been fortunate enough to have a good roll of the dice, and you land on a spot where you get bumped up another $200 already, so you can start buying those properties and putting little green houses and red hotels on them.

In the wheel of houses, in the Equal House system, the First House is the natural home to the first sign of Aries, so the Second House is home to Taurus, which is ruled by Venus. The Second House therefore has to do with things associated with Venus, such as the appreciation of beauty, including lovely, comfortable surroundings, fine clothing, artistic pleasures, and even an eye for attractive people. People with a loaded Second House are concerned about looks, including their own—hair care, skin, makeup, and fashion would all be important.

The Second House also shows the way we handle money, how good we are at making our way through the material world. It also shows our individual preference for a certain style of earning a living.

For example, the sign of Sagittarius on the Second House indicates an expansive, generous approach to money, which may be used to fund graduate school or seminary or special courses in religion, or to buy sporting goods or play the ponies. Individuals with this placement might plunder their coffers for their many travels abroad. In fact, they may make their living as a travel agent or guide, or a translator.

Beneficial planets in the Second House bring favorable circumstances to those lucky enough to have such placements—for example, having Jupiter here. The largest planet in the solar system placed in the Second House of property, monetary gains, and comfort suggests that the person was born into a comfortable situation or has the great good fortune to have a knack for making money or attracting wealth.

Take Donald Trump, for example. He has Jupiter and Neptune in the Second House. He grew up with a successful father, also a New York–based real-estate developer. But Fred Trump never reached the heights The Donald would enjoy, especially in the boom times of the eighties. Trump personified that larger-than-life, what-the-hell decade with his lavish lifestyle, love affairs, and somewhat cryptic deals.

Jupiter inspires other people's confidence, and Trump always seems to be able to get people to invest in his properties—perhaps because of the "Trump image"—when other less charismatic or lesser known individuals are turned down. In fact, with Neptune there, who knows how Trump and others like him get their money? Neptune in the Second

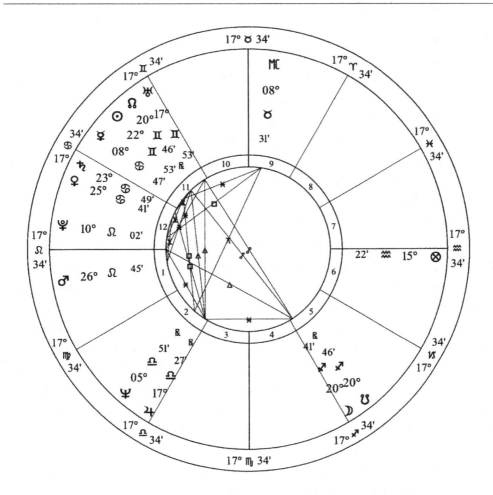

Donald Trump
June 14, 1946 / 9:51 a.m. Daylight Saving Time
Time Zone: 5 hours West
Queens, NY / Equal Houses

House has a quality of "smoke and mirrors," and I've always felt there was a bit of voodoo in Trump's high-stakes real estate endeavors.

Jupiter makes him lucky, and indeed it seems like someone is always there to bail him out. Plus now, as I'm writing this, Trump is a media celebrity, on the top of the pop-culture dungheap with the series *The Apprentice*.

That's also the Neptunian influence—television and celebrity are not the real world (no matter what the people behind the reality shows would like us to believe), and it is fitting that a person like Trump, with a Second-House Neptune, would capture the public's imagination with this kind of fairy tale.

When the Second House is activated in a person's chart, they need to be "involved in trying to create an environment around (themselves) which expresses (their) values, or in setting projects in motion which express them," according to River and Gillespie.[2]

Here is the downside to an activated Second House. Either a stellium of planets there or a challenging aspect can indicate a tendency toward indolence. Ruling-planet Venus loves comfort, but can also make certain compromises to ensure a certain level of material comfort is maintained. Too much emphasis on "stuff" (as George Carlin would say) could lead to an individual running up debts or staying in an unfulfilling job in order to pay the bills. (In a twist on the Seven Dwarfs, one humorous bumper sticker I saw read, "I Owe, I Owe, So Off to Work I Go.") Second-House planets evoke images of "the lady of the house," but in another way they could also point to "The Madam" or her employees. Don't prostitute yourself to keep up with the Joneses.

If the Second House has challenging aspects, or if Saturn is there, the person will have money issues or may have to work harder to enjoy the comforts it bestows easily on others. With Saturn, there may be karma involved. In a previous life, these people may have been manipulative with money or overly materialistic. In this lifetime, they have incarnated with these challenges in order to balance and reassess their value systems.

It might feel like a struggle to people with a Second-House Saturn, but they'll be more enlightened next time around with the knowledge they glean about the material world. What the heck—it's all just "stuff."

I recall a friend and client named John, with a Second-House Venus, in the sign of Libra. This unusual man, who is now deceased, seemed like he should have been a Kennedy—he loved to live like a rich person, and his tastes were always so refined. John had lived a middle-class-to-riches-to-rags kind of story. He had come back from Vietnam injured, confused, uneducated, and broke, but he landed on his feet beautifully, like the purebred Abyssinian cat he would purchase when his fortunes rose. Thanks to his considerable charm, he managed to marry an heiress to one of the country's large chemical companies, before the age of twenty-five.

He was too young for it to last, though. My friend and client received a generous divorce settlement, which he used to fund a high-rolling lifestyle. John had never been to college, was never really gainfully employed, and was only in his mid-twenties, but there he was, cruising around San Francisco in a nut-brown Mercedes convertible, with a chic apartment in North Beach. A friend taught him the business of running an upscale coffee shop long before the Starbucks empire existed—just because he liked John and saw his potential.

John never reached those heights again, but even when I knew him—when he was a lot more down and out—he took taxis everywhere, wore preppy, expensive shirts (which he always had laundered), and filled his third-floor walk-up apartment with antiques and art. He might have been running low on toothpaste and bathroom tissue, but there was frequently a bottle of champagne in the fridge.

People were always giving John things, including job offers, invitations to parties and intimate little dinners, great deals on jewelry, artwork, recorded music and musical instruments, food, clothing—and, unfortunately, drugs. That's what killed him.

There were many other factors in my late friend's chart that precipitated his self-destruction, including the fact that he had absolutely no earth signs in his chart to give him a good sense of grounding or roots. His family, who also gave him a great deal of emotional and financial support, suggest that he was troubled from an early age—which his experience in the war certainly didn't help.

But John's Venus in the Second House bestowed on him an unusual sense of grace, which included a love for art and music, a beautiful speaking voice, good looks, charm, and genuine kindness. And that is what those of us who loved him remember best.

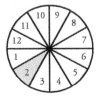

Second House: The natural house for Taurus, ruled by Venus, the Second House has to do with material possessions, money, generosity or greed, and inclinations toward ways of making money.

Planets in the Second House

Sun in the Second House

These people need to feel a sense of self-worth and can be overly focused on attaining personal power through possessions, money, and talents. Money comes and goes easily. They are generous and ambitious, but could also be extravagant, grasping, and possessive, which includes possessiveness with lovers and spouses.

Moon in the Second House

These folks have a desire to possess both money and material things for emotional security. This placement could bring many financial ups and downs. These individuals fluctuate between being careless and thrifty.

Mercury in the Second House

These people are quick-witted and versatile, with the ability to communicate to others through writing and speaking. They have financial skill, but need to apply it better, because money seems to slip through their fingers. The mind, however, is motivated toward making money. There is also a love for books and music.

Venus in the Second House

These folks have a natural understanding of finance, but also the ability to spend money faster than it comes in. They seem to magically attract money. Venus in the Second House indicates hidden creative talents.

Mars in the Second House

With this placement, money comes and goes and is less important than the development of the individual's talents. Emotional, with a strong sex drive, these folks are in touch with their sensuality and sundry physical pleasures. Watch for a tendency to link sex with power, or even money. In marriage, too much emphasis on material things and control of the finances could cause conflict. Since sex is so important, these individuals could throw this into the mix, too, using sex to get their way or withholding it to punish the partner. They could be the jealous type. Partners are sometimes treated like possessions, not human beings. Individuals with a Second-House Mars need to play fair and back away from materialism.

Jupiter in the Second House

This is a placement for financial success. These natives have confidence combined with optimism. This is a good position for speculations and ideas, which seem to work out magically thanks to strong intuitions. People with a Second-House Jupiter inspire trust and therefore often receive financial assistance from others to fund their ideas and investments. They enjoy their material possessions, but should guard against overextending themselves.

Saturn in the Second House

These individuals are thrifty, practical, and responsible. Sometimes their possessions bring worries rather than pleasures. They can offset this tendency by sharing with others. In past lives, they were too materialistic and have come into this incarnation to reassess their values. This placement doesn't necessarily deny money, but these people may have to work harder for it than they feel they deserve.

Uranus in the Second House

These folks are independent, emotional, and excitable. They earn their money in inventive ways. Unexpected changes in their financial condition may occur. They are not usually concerned about material things, but need money for the freedom it provides to pursue their adventures and ideas.

Neptune in the Second House

These folks are intuitive and imaginative, with great potential for psychic abilities. They are apt to have vivid dreams and an appreciation of beautiful objects. They seldom worry about money, which is just as well because finances can be complicated. This placement can make these individuals extremely generous or just as equally dishonest. If they are dishonest, they run the risk of loss through theft, fraud, or deception.

Pluto in the Second House

This is a great placement for financial ability. People with a Second-House Pluto have a keen sense of judgment and are patient, energetic, and talented. There is a desire for money and possessions, which might also include loved ones and friends. The best way to channel the energy of this placement is to share with others and use integrity in money matters.

1. George Carlin, *A Place for My Stuff* (New York: BMG Records, 1981).

2. Lindsay River and Sally Gillespie, *The Knot of Time* (New York: Harper & Row, 1987), pp. 226–7.

CHAPTER SIX

Third House:
Brothers, Sisters, and School Days

"What we have here is a failure to communicate."
—Cool Hand Luke

Recently I counted the number of magazines my husband and I subscribe to, and I think it's up to about fourteen. The number varies because subscriptions run out and we opt to not renew them, or we discover new ones and sign up, or I borrow them from the chiropractor's office, or I pick up the free ones, especially anything New Age-oriented. We get everything from serious publications with a long history of excellence, such as *The New Yorker*, to trade publications, such as *Editor & Publisher*, the *Columbia Journalism Review*, and *Mad* magazine.

Since we both work for newspapers, there are usually lots of those around too, especially on Sundays. That's not to mention the couple thousand books we own. Did I mention that we're both Geminis? My husband has four signs in Gemini, so that pretty much explains his obsession with the written word. But I also have three signs in the Third House, which means that my love for words, books, and communications is a given.

Ruled by Mercury and associated with Gemini, the Third House is the natural place for the sign of the Twins. Pertaining to communications and learning, especially early education, the Third House is where the young soul starts to discover the world around her. If the Second House was where she had the good (or bad) fortune to land, the Third House suggests the child starting to strike out on her own—not too far, as with the Ninth House, which has to do with foreign travel and wanderlust, but far enough to get a feel for what the neighborhood is like.

Indeed, the Third House also has to do with neighbors and immediate surroundings—everyday flotsam and jetsam, like the daily newspaper or the mail. (I love the U.S. Mail and go through withdrawal when the mailbox is empty.) In addition, it tells us how a person might learn, her mental capacity, as well as how she gets around, since the Third House is also connected with mobility.

A powerful planet (such as the Sun or Moon) or a group of planets in the Third House means you have a lifelong student on your hands. Whether it's signing up for night school or being addicted to PBS, strong Third-House folks never stop learning. And isn't that a great quality to have?

There is evidence that continuing to acquire new skills as we age keeps the demonic forces of depression at bay and may even stimulate the centers of the brain that control Alzheimer's disease. For the elderly, as well as those of us who are getting up there in age, doing word games or crossword puzzles is like calisthenics for the brain.

As I'm writing this, the great French photographer Henri Cartier-Bresson has recently passed away at age ninety-five. I have a theory that photographers live especially long because they are constantly in the process of looking—they delight in seeing new things all the time. In an interview with Charlie Rose, Cartier-Bresson lit up when he started to look at his interviewer's face the way a photographer would. He had been serious and a little quiet, but when he was "thinking in pictures"—seeing the angles and details of Charlie Rose's face—you could almost hear the synapses popping. Photographers André Kertész, Alfred Eisenstaedt, Irving Penn, Alfred Stieglitz, and Richard Avedon all lived to a ripe old age. Their minds were wide-awake, their eyes open—evidence that curiosity and wonder don't cease when one gets older.

Learning, seeing the world through the eyes of a child, is truly a gift, one that a well-aspected, powerful Third House bestows.

The sign on the cusp of this house will tell a lot about the "style" in which a person learns, applies his or her mental abilities and communications skills, and interacts with neighbors and the community.

A client of mine named Adam has Leo on the Third House, with the Moon and Venus there, and indeed, he does express himself frequently. I only met him once or twice, about seven years ago, but he still sends an e-mail at least once a week. He's a composer, screenwriter, humorist, and "part-time mystic," and he likes to send his original CDs and various tapes of radio programs to me in the mail. (See, he likes the mail too.) That's his Leo Moon conjunct Venus in the Third House—he is generous with his communications.

And confident. Sometimes his missives border on being overblown and a teensy bit opinionated (that's Leo). He once wrote a note expressing his opinion that a certain guitarist was the Antichrist, which kind of offended me, until I understood that this was his sense of humor.

We had a misunderstanding—a communications breakdown—which is also a telltale sign of the Moon in the Third House. The Moon is a watery entity and doesn't feel quite at home in this house, ruled by quixotic Mercury and the natural place for airy Gemini. Having the Moon here sometimes clouds communications and, for better or worse, colors them with emotions. This makes for a wonderful composer of music and also a writer who can communicate with a certain amount of depth, but everyday interactions can also go awry when feelings are hurt.

If there are challenging aspects to Third-House planets, there may be issues of boundaries, which trigger negative emotions and have to be dealt with. A person's Third-House Moon may square a Twelfth-House Mars, "hiding" his confidence (Mars) and blocking his spontaneous sense of expression. Perhaps he won't stand up for himself and thus will be taken advantage of. Or he will refrain from expressing emotions until they are so tamped down that they come out in explosive, unpleasant, unproductive ways.

Interestingly, the Moon in the Third House also can indicate psychic ability in an individual. This could be the placement for someone skilled in "automatic writing" or working as a medium, receiving and transmitting messages from beyond. I don't know if Adam is psychic, but I know he enjoys contemplating such phenomena. He sends everyone on his

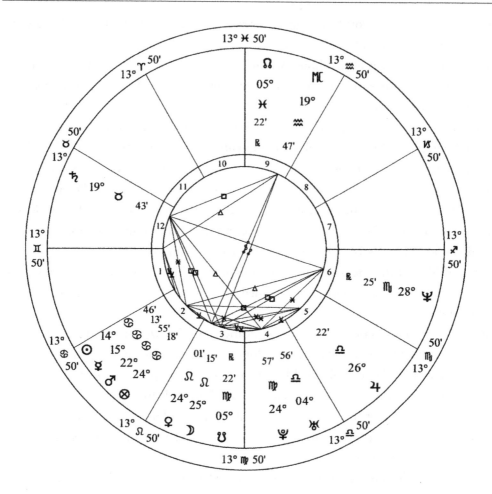

Adam
July 7, 1970 / 3:30 a.m. Daylight Saving Time
Time Zone: 5 hours West
Philadelphia, PA / Equal Houses

e-mail list updates about "incidences of synchronicity" he's encountered, dreams he thinks we would all enjoy, and anything about Carl Jung.

"If the Third House is emphasized by the Sun, Moon, or a cluster of planets, there is usually a high priority on the acquisition of new skills, continuing learning and on communication in the person's life," say River and Gillespie. "She may excel as a public speaker or a journalist, or work with books as a bookseller, editor or librarian. Third House Sun, Moon, Mercury or Uranus in particular, may be the mark of a writer."[1]

A challenging aspect (such as a square or opposition) to a planet in the Third House could indicate indicate blockage of mobility, since the Third House has to do with transportation. River and Gillespie note that the Third House is of special importance in the charts of people with disabilities. If a person's mobility is blocked or her communication ability is impaired (a speech impediment, for example), it's important that she have plenty of short trips, access to news and current events, chats with the neighbors, and exchanges of information—all things having to do with the Third House.

I enumerate the magazines and other things to illustrate how much a Mercurial person with an activated Third House (or my spouse, with all the Gemini in his chart) needs new information, like the kind that comes in the form of newspapers and magazines.

Last, but certainly not least, the Third House describes the kind of people who surround a person in youth. These are not the people you choose later in life or to partner with in marriage, but those you have been "assigned to" by the angelic realms, such as brothers and sisters. Past lives and reincarnation studies teach that you "choose" the people you incarnate with, in order to learn important soul lessons.

Sometimes these will be joyous reunions of compatible souls or helpmates from a previous life, and the sibling relationship will be a pleasant one—a true lifelong friendship. However, with challenging aspects to Third-House planets, there will be issues to be resolved with brothers and sisters, and sometimes cousins—but more often siblings.

I have a friend and client named Nancy, with her Moon in the Third House square to Mars and Venus, who has become an enigma to her extended family, separating herself from a boisterous gang of siblings, cousins, aunts, and uncles. Nancy and her older sister Jean have a strained relationship, as might be expected for someone with challenging aspects to the Third House. Nancy has given up the hope that her family might "hear" her side of story, about how Jean bullies her, and so has retreated.

The problem is that Jean had issues of her own from an early age, including some physical problems that brought her a lot of attention. She certainly overcame whatever weaknesses she had as a baby and grew into a . . . loudmouth. You can hear Jean before you see her. She simply overshadowed and drowned out her younger sister, and also interrupted and ridiculed her to the level of verbal abuse. I witnessed her little "digs," which over the years really hurt Nancy, who always struck me as more retiring and thoughtful—but not a weak person. I don't think Nancy got a lot of support from her parents, who preferred to remain neutral about the hostilities.

Nancy, born on the cusp of Leo and Virgo, has a lot of pride and just wouldn't succumb to her bullying sister. The family didn't "hear" how much this troubled her and never stepped in to support her. So, Nancy moved across the country, and no one in the extended family sees her. Perhaps she is being too rigid about her big-mouth sister. If this is a karmic lesson, maybe the best approach would be to ignore or laugh about it—the Smothers Brothers have made a fortune joking about sibling rivalry.

On the other hand, the karma could be for Nancy to learn to draw emotional boundaries (the Moon), to be assertive and stand up to her sister. That hasn't happened, though. Perhaps it is too painful—she needed to feel loved by her sister and really took her sibling's chilliness and domination to heart. And indeed, it takes two to tango. I don't know how far or how much Nancy has tried to reach out to her sister, or vice versa. Instead, she seems to be very involved with her church, which brings her the familiar feeling she lacked among her own "tribe."

I'm sure this story of the two sisters resonates with many people who have challenging aspects to the Third House. With such issues, the best way to handle things is always to keep an open line of communication. And remember, everything is in divine order. There must be something to learn from the struggle.

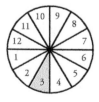 *Third House:* The natural house for Gemini and ruled by Mercury, the Third House has to do with brothers and sisters, cousins, childhood friends, neighbors, early education, your neighborhood, short journeys and methods of transportation, communications, mental ability, capacity for learning, newspapers, magazines, mail, and other daily pleasantries.

Planets in the Third House

Sun in the Third House

With this placement, there is a deep desire to know and understand through concrete knowledge or scientific proof. Therefore, these folks could be skeptical, especially of spiritual information. They can be domineering and impatient, which could lead to trouble with relatives and neighbors (or siblings and playmates in childhood). There is a strong need to learn, communicate, and show off their knowledge.

Moon in the Third House

Emotions may rule the mind of a person with a Third-House Moon, so here is another instance where understanding how to calm one's "monkey mind" through cognitive behavioral therapy or meditation can be beneficial. These individuals prefer a pleasant environment, especially in the workplace, and dislike routine. They also prefer to learn through listening or experience rather than studying a book, although they are curious and enjoy taking in new information. They need it, in fact. They are also lifelong students, willing to learn new skills and gather information and keep the creative juices going into old age.

I once interviewed Jon Katz, the author and dog-training expert who frequently writes about his relationships with animals. Talking about his book *The Dogs of Bedlam Farm*, he said that, in late middle age, he took on the challenge of running a remote farm and training several Border collies to keep "mind death" at bay. "I watched people in late middle age cease to be interested in anything," he said. "That's one of the reasons I took on the farm. In late middle age, I figure you have a decision to make. Will you continue to learn and grow, or will you settle down and not change? A lot of my friends think I'm crazy, but I look at them and they've become set in their ways and just talk about the old days. They're not doing or learning anything new. I call this 'the first death,' when you close the door to new possibilities. Then comes the death of the body. I fear the first kind more than the second." That's a good summation and a good way to understand the Third-House Moon's continuing curiosity about the world.

Mercury in the Third House

With Mercury in this house, ideas flow freely, combined with the stick-to-it-tiveness to bring things to completion. This is a placement for a versatile, studious, adaptable, clever individual who might find rewarding work in teaching, especially in the lower grades. With challenging aspects, the person could be a dilettante, or work could be hampered by a tendency to worry, particularly about relatives.

Venus in the Third House

Unless there are challenging aspects, this is a beneficial placement, bringing a pleasant personality, artistic and communication abilities, and a tendency to find oneself in harmonious surroundings and relationships, especially with relatives and neighbors. These folks enjoy the excitement of fast-moving forms of transportation, such as motorcycles or sports cars or galloping horses. If Venus has a hard aspect—for example, if the planet is squared by Mars or Uranus—they should be extra careful in speeding vehicles, since there is a possibility of accidents. These people love to travel and are great diplomats because they abhor arguments.

Mars in the Third House

These folks have an abundance of mental energy and are enthusiastic and determined. This position could indicate problems in the childhood home environment because of quarrels, perhaps with siblings or playmates, which could lay the groundwork for a high-strung personality. Such people would need to be taught to be more deliberate and analytical in their thinking, because impulsiveness can bring troubles.

Jupiter in the Third House

Jupiter here indicates mental restlessness that might need to be harnessed, or the person could become too scattered. With proper application and if well aspected, this is the placement for an expansive, philosophical mind, with an ability to grasp a number of different subject matters and tie them in together. A great love for learning persists throughout life, and these people make wonderful teachers or speakers. An occupation where they juggle a number of tasks or move around physically would be beneficial, as these individuals hate routine.

Saturn in the Third House

Childhood may have been a little lonely, perhaps because these folks were left alone or didn't receive enough attention. They can grow up to believe they don't "deserve" to have friends or take part in social situations, which could lead to feelings of depression. On the other hand, this is an excellent placement for people who enjoy long-term, exacting projects. They are hard-working and have orderly minds and good mental retention.

Uranus in the Third House

These individuals are rebels and roamers and are dissatisfied with routine. They hate the mundaneness of home life, especially within a dysfunctional family. Therefore, off they go, picking up and leaving in search of the perfect place or group of strangers who can be a surrogate family. Their wanderlust makes them interesting speakers and writers. They're inventive, original, independent, and creative—but don't expect them to make a commitment to routine.

Neptune in the Third House

This placement indicates the potential for emotional struggles in early childhood and in the family of origin, most likely with the siblings, which can hurt sometimes. There is karmic energy about relationships at work here. Perhaps the karmic lesson of those with a Third-House Neptune is to stand up for themselves or learn to draw boundaries, and they might have to "practice" on their siblings and family. These struggles can be overcome, especially as these individuals grow up and gain a broader perspective, and also find more like-minded friends outside of the family. This placement also brings many gifts, including artistic, intuitive, and psychic abilities. These folks have interesting dreams, too, but need to watch out for obsessions.

Pluto in the Third House

These individuals are versatile, original, and inspired, with a keen ability to evaluate situations and sniff out shady, unreliable people. They have inquisitive minds and good powers of concentration but may be chewing on inner turmoil about deeper meaning—their souls need to seek answers to thorny questions. Therefore, they can become depressed if there isn't an outlet of creative expression or a sympathetic ear, such as a therapist or counselor. In fact, these people make good counselors, because of their depth, insight, and ability to communicate.

---

1. Lindsay River and Sally Gillespie, *The Knot of Time* (New York: Harper & Row, 1987), pp. 228–9.

CHAPTER SEVEN

Fourth House: Family Affairs

Much of the emphasis of the Fourth House is on the concept of home, family, and roots. It's an interesting topic of discussion in an age when people move around and away from their families of origin, change jobs, and seem much more rootless than in previous times. Still, there is usually one place in our unconscious where we need to feel centered, as though we have put down roots psychologically, if not literally. No matter how much an individual likes to travel, it's necessary to establish some kind of space that feels safe and comforting.

Without this feeling of being grounded, individuals tend to have a deep longing for connection, replacing this bond with a substitute—sometimes falling into bad habits, such as abusing drugs and alcohol, sexual addictions, overspending, or even working too much. I think this rootlessness may be one of the reasons this nation has seen a rise in violence, materialism, and crimes committed by children. We're losing touch with our personal family history, ancestry, and heritage, and as a society we're deviating more and more from cultural and societal traditions. All of these are issues governed by the Fourth House.

Sometimes called the House of the Mother, Parent, or Nurturer, the Fourth House represents the place where the young soul has grown enough to know his physical and basic psychological ways of presenting himself (First House), material resources (Second House), and immediate environment (Third House). Now the individual begins to get a sense of "self," feels rooted and more confident, especially if the person has healthy nurturing and encouragement from the parents, particularly the mother.

Because it is associated with heritage and roots (and in Western society our lineage is passed down through the males), the Fourth House is sometimes connected with the father. However, since it is the natural placement for the sign of Cancer and is ruled by the watery, feminine Moon, I feel the mother has more resonance in the Fourth House.

Mother—as an individual and as an archetype—is very, very important to anyone with an activated Fourth House, especially if the sign on the cusp of the house is a water sign. Any grouping of planets in the Fourth House, especially if there are challenging aspects, points to some issues with the mother, usually with karmic ties that need to be explored and resolved.

Mars here, especially, often indicates problems with Mom. The Fourth House is the bottom of the chart, and Mars never likes to be on the bottom (or at the end) of anything. The natural Martian energy and spontaneity will be subdued somehow. Perhaps the individual will be overshadowed by an overbearing, narcissistic, unloving mother. Or Mom may have been ill when the individual was growing up—she may have even died. The child with a Fourth-House Mars may have had to take care of the mother, to be the parent in the home. Or, in our modern culture, this could be a working mom, just too busy to give the kind of love the individual requires. The fire of the Red Planet requires a lot of fuel for the heart, and with this position, the mother may have had a short supply.

The downsides of a Fourth-House Mars could be a feeling of frustration and a sense of abandonment. The individual wonders if she is worthy of love. All of this carries over into adulthood, where grown-up relationships suffer. In marriage, the person might reenact the chaos of her childhood home. A man with a challenging Fourth-House Mars could hold inside the anger from life with Mom for years after childhood, until it explodes into adult violence.

There is also a sense of abandonment, of never feeling safe, and then not wanting to get close to others emotionally because of this. With therapy, though, this can be circumvented and understood. We are all worthy of loving another, and we are all equally worthy of receiving love.

To a person working through the issues of an unloving parent, reframing the relationship is one way to understand, logically, what went wrong. As children, we look upon our parents as gods and goddesses, all-powerful people with all the answers. As we mature, we understand that they are flawed human beings, just like we are. If we have children of our own, we learn how difficult it is to raise a family and not make some mistakes. (How many times have we heard the jokes about "wait until you have children of your own"?) Most of all, we come to understand that the lack of proper parenting was not our fault.

We know from the discussion of the *Imum Coeli* in chapter 2 that the Fourth House is also where we can find untapped resources and buried treasure. So, if we have a heavy planet poorly aspected in the Fourth House, it might mean that we are not best friends with Mother, nor do we feel particularly close to our family of origin. This situation may motivate us to become strong and independent, and eventually find another "family" or "home" with nonrejecting people more like ourselves.

The possibility of family dysfunction is one of the bleaker aspects of the Fourth House, but there are many positive things about finding planets here. Mostly, this position is about roots, heritage, and stability, which bring owning land and real estate into the picture. The Sun in the Fourth House or Leo on the Fourth-House cusp makes a person particularly keen on owning property and real estate. It makes the Leo individual feel better about himself, and he will most likely turn the place into a palace, inviting in masses of company to be entertained in high style.

Saturn in the Fourth House is a placement that could indicate either a deathly, irrational fear of unemployment and homelessness (leftover residue from a difficult, impoverished past life) or else a strong belief in home and that nebulous phrase "family values."

This is usually a good thing, a positive place for Saturn. "Tribes" hanging in there together and giving each other support is refreshing in this age of fractured families. The flip side is that overidentification with the tribe can impede an individual's self-expression. Those with a Fourth-House Saturn may put their personal dreams on hold in order to stay in line with what the family expects of them. Men (and women now) may go into the family business, for example, not out of interest but obligation. This may be especially true if there is an ambitious, business-oriented father, which is likely with this Saturn position.

Happily, people with Saturn in the Fourth have the wherewithal to pursue their interests, and with the long life this placement suggests, they may get to do so in their more mature years. Just as with the Sun in the Fourth House, this placement suggests that the person will not move too far from home.

Interestingly, one person in the spotlight who has stayed close to home—and, in fact, made a fortune out of writing songs about his hometown roots and values—is Bruce Springsteen. Hey, I'm from New Jersey. Every day we are required to mention Bruce Springsteen at least once.

The Sun, Neptune, and Mercury in the Fourth House all help give The Boss an extra oomph to his love for the home—at least, that's what his persona is all about. But it may be an apt description of the real Springsteen, too, who really does have a residence at the Jersey Shore in the beautiful town of Rumson, not too far from his hometown of Freehold and from the Asbury Park beaches and boardwalks he wrote about.

After a rocky marriage to model and actress Julianne Phillips, Springsteen fell for a Jersey girl, Patti Scialfa, who grew up going to those same beaches, sang in the same seaside clubs, and probably hung with the same bohemians and bay rats as Bruce.

It's also interesting to note that Bruce's star rose when he reconnected with the E Street Band. He had cut them loose in the late 1980s to record a couple of unheralded albums, and then reformed the band to make *The Rising*, the excellent 2002 release, much of which reflects Springsteen's feelings and impressions of the September 11 terrorist attacks. He brings the tragic event right down to the home front, even to the intimacy of the bedroom, with "You're Missing." Many people felt more healed by Bruce's music about 9/11 than any speeches our politicians could offer. He has that ability—even at the apex of stardom—to connect with so many fans in the United States and around the world. Why? And why has he lasted for so long in the music business?

One of the answers may lie in his powerful Fourth House. Bruce Springsteen most likely feels a loyalty to his home and his roots, and knows instinctively how to convey that in words (Mercury) and music. He also has a strong, creative Fifth House, which has bestowed many gifts on The Boss.

No, life is not all about rich people and glamour. There are many more of us regular folks out here than there are people in the top tax bracket. With all his fame, Springsteen still manages to maintain a connection with the average person, by capturing the poetry of the ordinary moments in family, home, and individual life.

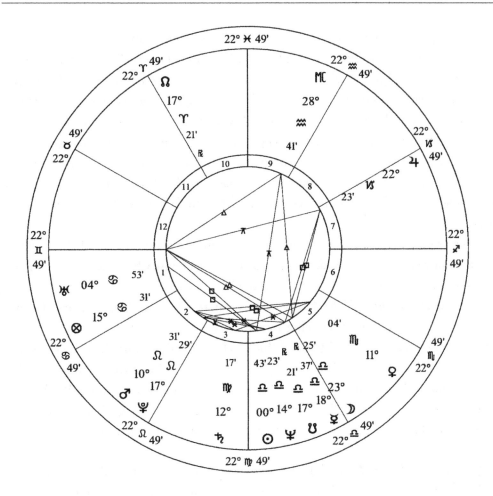

Bruce Springsteen
September 23, 1949 / 10:50 p.m. Daylight Saving Time
Time Zone: 5 hours West
Freehold, NJ / Equal Houses

"He is, to put it simply, a story teller, and in straining to make his stories credible he uses classic techniques," writes Simon Frith in his essay "The Real Thing—Bruce Springsteen."[1]

"Springsteen's songs, like Zola's fictions, are almost exclusively concerned with the working class, with the effects of poverty and uncertainty, the consequences of weakness and crime, they travel through the murky reality of the American dream; they contrast Utopian impulses with people's lack of opportunity to do much more than get by . . . There's a . . . tradition of artists as the common man, pitching truth against urban deceit, pioneer values against bureaucratic routines. This tradition (Mark Twain to Woody Guthrie, Jack Kerouac to Creedence Clearwater Revival) lies behind Springsteen's message and his image."[2]

I believe he's real. I live just forty-five minutes from the real E Street in Belmar, where one of the musician's mothers lived. We drive by the actual house where the band once practiced, and there really is a Tenth Avenue Freeze-Out (an ice cream shop). Madame Marie, the fortuneteller from *4th of July: Asbury Park*, is real, too. In fact, she just returned to her little place on the Boardwalk after being away for many years.[3]

Springsteen has an authenticity that, I think, is linked with his busy Fourth House. For those of us who may not have had a happy home, who feel disconnected from our tribe, his words and music touch that need to be rooted, to relate to something. By the way, Springsteen rarely writes about his own mother, although the moving tribute "The Wish" appears on the 1998 compilation. He writes frequently about his father, though.

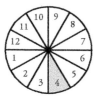 *Fourth House:* The natural home for Cancer and ruled by the Moon, the Fourth House governs personal foundations, inner emotional security and self-image, the individual's mother and home, as well as conditions at the end of life.

Planets in the Fourth House

Sun in the Fourth House

Mom lurks in the background here, throughout these individuals' lives. Without a healthy foundation, they may be filled with self-doubt. In order to toe the "maternal" line (they never really cut the cord), they have a tendency to be conservative. But they make committed homebodies, and are proud of this.

Moon in the Fourth House

This placement indicates a change of residence, or just redecorating the interiors or renovating an existing home, all of which is therapeutic. This is how these folks seek to find themselves, to find security—building or finding the perfect nest alleviates their feelings of insecurity, which may relate to their relationships with their mothers. Mom plays a strong role, positive or negative, throughout these people's lives.

Mercury in the Fourth House

The original homeschoolers, these people love to study, but prefer to do it in their own environment. If they can live close to a school or, ideally, teach and live on campus, they're in heaven. Students for life, they may move many times, searching for the perfect residence.

Venus in the Fourth House

These folks desire to make their "nest" into a beautiful and welcoming environment for friends, family, and strangers. They genuinely enjoy people and have a great love for family and children. The Fourth House governs end-of-life conditions, so old age will be comfortable unless there are very challenging aspects or other factors in the chart.

Mars in the Fourth House

These scrappy, strong folks have a desire for freedom from an early age, yet paradoxically also crave security and a home of their own. They have to make peace with this conflict between independence and a nesting nature, or they will be antagonistic and argumentative on the homefront.

Jupiter in the Fourth House

These individuals get luckier and wealthier as they get older, perhaps from an inheritance. There are links to the parents that shape their character throughout their lives. These are not urban, studio-apartment dwellers—they need too much space. Generous and hospitable, they need a large, comfortable home, and surely must love the trend of fourteen-room McMansions, which allow them to host the entire family.

Saturn in the Fourth House

Here we again find karmic issues with the parents, probably more with the mother than the father. With this placement, there may be some residual fears—due to past-life memories—of a struggle to make ends meet, of not having a roof over one's head. Perhaps these individuals lived through famine or a war in a previous life. In this life, then, they could stay tied to their family of origin for financial stability or work in a family business that doesn't properly feed the soul. On the other hand, these people are loyal to their family of origin and will be the "family rock" in times of crisis, stepping in to handle the most difficult situations. They like to collect things. At best, they will collect fine antiques, particularly furniture. At worst, they could be pack rats, saving every newspaper, magazine, and paper bag.

Uranus in the Fourth House

This placement indicates a love-hate relationship with the home and a unique (read: "strange") relationship with the mother. These folks may have to move many times in their young lives, which aggravates an innate sense of rootlessness and contributes to their "commitment phobia" as adults. On the other hand, they could make peace with their wanderlust, and be old hippie-gypsies, with tales from the four corners and various people of the world. They could also cultivate an interest in metaphysics.

Neptune in the Fourth House

People with this placement have a great love for nature and sometimes long to have a home in the woods or another natural setting. They can eschew mainstream living to roost like mountain men or women in a camplike situation, in a trailer or RV or even a tent. Being near water is important to them. Home ownership might be delayed (they don't mind renting or sharing space with roommates), but when they do establish a home, those with a Fourth-House Neptune will "bring nature inside," with lavish plants, fountains or pools, pets, and lovely works of art. Home life in early childhood may have been chaotic, which is one of the reasons these people don't mind putting off home ownership. They'd rather stay in touch with the soothing, restorative powers of nature.

Pluto in the Fourth House

These intuitive, imaginative, passionate people have a strong desire for love and security. Family is important to them, but if there is dysfunction or a lack of love in the childhood home, they will explore ways to establish a family or tribe of their own with like-minded, sympathetic friends. The relationship to the mother is profoundly important, since Pluto, with its mythic connection to the underground, creates the deepest, most powerful emotions, and the Fourth House is naturally connected with the Moon and all things maternal. An unkind mother could make for individuals who hold the hurt inside and fume throughout childhood, until they're older and anger bursts from them with a kind of volcanic power. Those with a Fourth-House Pluto could feel a pull between loyalty to the home and a desire to see the world. They could also be quite skilled in dealing with real estate.

1. Simon Frith, "The Real Thing—Bruce Springsteen," from *Music for Pleasure: Essays in the Sociology of Pop,* reprinted in *Racing in the Street: The Bruce Springsteen Reader* (New York: Penguin, 2004).

2. Ibid., pp. 136–9.

3. I heard about this on a local radio station, and went over to the Asbury Park, New Jersey, Boardwalk, and voilà—there was Madame Marie, in the flesh. She was a little snarly.

CHAPTER EIGHT

Fifth House: Crazy Love

I won a banana-seat bicycle once, in a summertime raffle sponsored by my hometown's Democratic Society. My grandmother, a staunch Republican who used to keep pictures of Barry Goldwater and Richard Nixon on her wall, thought that I should probably give the bicycle back—no supporting those left-wing radicals!

That was in 1971 and that was probably the last thing I won by sheer luck. I have sweated and toiled over musical and written accomplishments and was deservedly the employee of the month at one job where I worked something like sixty hours a week. But as far as lotteries and other games of chance go, forget it. My father buys lottery tickets for our Christmas stockings; it's been a tradition for years. Have I ever won anything? Well, I think I won two dollars once about fifteen years ago. I wish my father would just give me twenty bucks instead of buying twenty dollars' worth of lottery tickets. At least I could go do something with it.

Really, I don't have much luck in games of chance. For me, most everything has to be earned. I'm the person who consistently drops the bread butter side down.

I suspect that's partially because I have Saturn in the Fifth House, the Happy House, the position of creativity and talent, imagination, romance, pleasure, children, and luck. Not me—Saturn makes me work my tail off for everything. But that's the bleak side of the Fifth House, which is usually all about bestowing blessings on those who have planets there.

Associated with Leo and the Sun, an individual with an activated or crowded Fifth House is probably enjoying life.

The fiery planets, in particular, like to be in the Fifth House, where the energy shines like the sun. Mars in the Fifth, especially, indicates a person passionate about self-expression, with enough vitality to follow through on creative projects. As children, these folks may be prodigies (and sexually precocious, too) and thus need understanding parents who will nurture their extraordinary talents. Fortunately, parents of this generation are tuned in to the creative needs of their children more so than previous generations, who believed children should be seen and not heard.

Fifth-House planets indicate courage, physical strength, and a lot of activity, which could be overwhelming to new parents, less-active siblings and playmates, or inexperienced teachers. If they can channel that strength and courage into adulthood, these individuals might grow into superb athletes.

A busy Fifth House is an indicator of creative talent in the form of entertainment, although the more charts I look at, the more it seems like sports stars have something going on in the Fifth House. Muhammad Ali, Shaquille O'Neal, and Pete Rose all have planets in the Fifth. Pete Rose has Neptune there too, which, interestingly, is also an indication of a love for gambling.

Indeed, sports stars are becoming what movie stars once were in our culture, and the sports industry itself is getting bigger and bigger all the time. Even sports for children are big business, where much time is dedicated. Parents who have young athletes can attest to this. This resonates with one of the downsides of the Fifth House. With all this attention to the special talents a loaded Fifth House can bring, the individual can become too self-absorbed—there can be too much concentration and time spent in individual creative efforts.

A client of mine had a husband with a huge talent and love for the piano who practiced constantly. Outsiders gushed over his talent and told the woman how lucky she was to be married to such a great musician.

But it wasn't like that. Not only did the pianist expect her to do everything around the house and with the family while he played his instrument, he neglected her as well. I'm not sure he worked, either.

He had the Sun in the Fifth House, and potentially, the warmth of the Sun here could have overcome the man's driven quality and made him see what he was doing to his family. Perhaps if the wife had been more adamant or had insisted the pianist go for therapy, he would have realized that his family needed him as a father and a husband as much as the world needed a great musician.

Fifth-House folks really are warm, especially with positive planetary placements here, and they have a great capacity for love.

Fiery planets in the Fifth House usually mean love for and a way with children. Jupiter here (or Sagittarius on the cusp) makes great teachers and coaches of young people. These individuals bring the expansiveness of the largest planet into young people's lives, encouraging them to be all they can be. Taken too far, these individuals can be like stage mothers or the most obsessed soccer mom you know—pushing their children to the point where it's not fun for the little ones anymore. Or they could feel their own egos inflated through their children's achievements, neglecting their own soul's growth in order to have the best darn kiddies in the school. But those are extremes.

My friend Marghie's chart shows the more positive aspects of Jupiter in the Fifth House. Fifth-House planets bring a childlike quality to the individual, as well as a love for children, which my friend personifies.

Her young niece and nephew are her pals. She really relates to them and understands how their imaginations work. In the summer, in true Fifth-House form, she's on the beach early in the season with her young friends. I don't know who has more fun making sand castles. One time she got badly sunburned because she was at the beach for hours with a gaggle of children, riding the waves of their energy.

Bounty and luck with children can also be taken literally, and the Fifth House brings a real potential for reproduction. These folks are surprisingly precocious with their sexuality. Love affairs are very important to them, remember, and these people are naturally quite physical. Put the two together, and they might have a surprise bundle of joy in their hands. If you have children with an activated Fifth House, you might be wise to tell them about the birds and bees early on, or just keep a hawk eye on them. They love to be in love, and

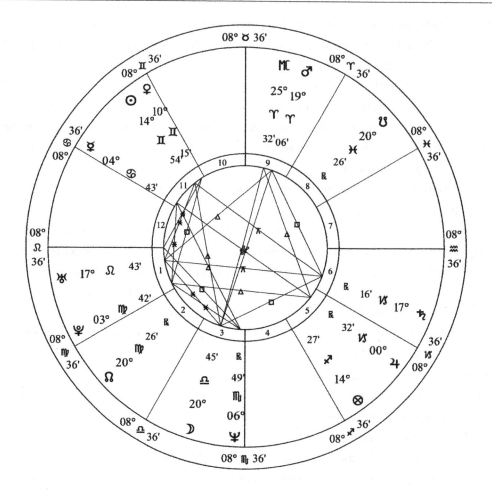

Marghie
June 5, 1960 / 9:30 a.m. Daylight Saving Time
Time Zone: 6 hours West
Waukegan, IL / Equal Houses

like to "get busy" and show their enthusiasm and warmth physically. They could be overwhelmed by passion and respond sexually in a relationship before the other person has made a commitment—or even taken them out on a date. They may lack the caution or self-restraint to consider the "protocol" of relationships.

A current trend among young people is the concept of "friends with benefits," which means girls and guys are supposedly "just friends," but the guys expect the girls to give them sex now too. That's the negative side of the Fifth House. Parents should talk wisely and openly about the physical expressions of love and the real dangers that can be out there in the form of sexually transmitted diseases. The sex drive is especially strong with Mars here.

On the other hand, with wise counsel, a young Fifth-House person's "love jones" can be channeled into creative pursuits or healthy physical activity, such as yoga, dance, or martial arts.

Sometimes, in the bleakest circumstances, a broken heart or thwarted love affair could cause a Fifth-House person to become violent or turn the anger inward, into depression.

The Moon in the Fifth House, especially, can make the heart fragile when it comes to love affairs. Romance might mean emotionally charged, painful experiences. These individuals would do well to learn how to balance their tender feelings with clear thinking, protecting themselves from vulnerability. The Moon in the Fifth House also points to sensitivity regarding creative matters, so if these individuals do become creative artists, they should develop a tough skin to deal with critics.

Challenging aspects to Fifth-House planets, or having cranky old Saturn here, can delay children. Sometimes there is karma involved—perhaps these folks had many children in a previous life, or perhaps they died in childbirth and the subconscious fear is that pregnancy will bring death or denial of their own creative potential. Some people just don't make good parents. Saturn here could make these natives real taskmasters with their children, making it more like an employer-employee relationship. They could have a cold streak, and there will not be enough love to go around if children come into their lives. Or, more positively, pregnancy may not occur until later in life.

If there are problems with children, remember that everything is in divine order. Maybe the universe is sending some of us a message. There are other ways to be a "parent" to the world, and many other roads of creative expression.

If you find Saturn in the Fifth House, consider a past-life regression to find out what the deeper issues might be.

Saturn here also makes these natives work really hard to get their creative projects off the ground. They might be reluctant to even try an artistic endeavor, for fear of criticism or because they think they have to be perfect.

To deny creativity is to deny the deepest, truest essence of ourselves, the spark that fuels our lives, the way the Creator flows through all our hearts. So we may not all be van Goghs or Hemingways—there are many other ways to be creative, such as cooking, sewing, decorating, gardening, or even just singing along to the radio. The arts are there for all of us to enjoy, and a poetic experience can happen anywhere, including the produce aisle of the grocery store. Cultivating awareness—seeing the world through the eyes of a child—is one way to unclog a blocked-up Fifth House. Then, living with our senses open, being wide-awake, is an act of creativity in itself. Life becomes a work of art.

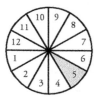 ***Fifth House:*** The Happy House is the natural place for Leo and is ruled by the Sun. It governs parties, pleasures, sports, creativity, love affairs, gambling, and speculation.

Planets in the Fifth House

Sun in the Fifth House

This placement is similar to the Sun in Leo, and is ideal for expressing one's innate creativity. Actors, rock stars, and athletes often have their Sun here, or else these are people who admire and aspire to the theater or the sports arena. Frustration with ambition could make these folks arrogant. Otherwise, they enjoy life to the hilt, especially artistic pursuits.

Moon in the Fifth House

These folks need to be the center of attention, similar to those with the Moon in Leo. They are indeed charming, good social strokers, artistic, and regal, but can be maddening with their elitism and drama-queen antics. They are truly affectionate with their children, however, and with lovers.

Mercury in the Fifth House

With this placement, romance must be balanced between the heart, the genitals, and the mind. Communication drives these people's intimate relationships. They have a great need for their original thoughts to be heard and to prove their intelligence. They make talented writers, speakers, and teachers—especially anything that involves coaching others to be the best they can be.

Venus in the Fifth House

Unless it is poorly aspected, this is another good placement for Venus, filled with creative expression and talents that may even be appreciated by the outside world. But if Venus is squared by masculine Mars, for example, the individual could seesaw between an easygoing, attractive nature and argumentativeness and a need to dominate. These people are often attractive to the opposite sex. Bruce Springsteen has and Marlena Dietrich had this placement. Enough said.

Mars in the Fifth House

With this placement you'll find lovers of sports, speculation, and entrepreneurial activities. These people are loyal and warm, with leadership abilities. There may, however, be karma with their children. They are balancing some thorny issues—specifically related to offspring—from previous lives.

Jupiter in the Fifth House

Jupiter in the Happy House is another fine placement. These folks are genuinely concerned with and affectionate toward children. They have a need to express themselves creatively, perhaps with their efforts going toward the greater good, such as benefit concerts or performances. Jupiter has to do with expansion and usually brings luck, but these people should watch out for too much "expansiveness" (spending) when it comes to gambling or running up debts.

Saturn in the Fifth House

Since Saturn is the planet of structure and limitations, and the Fifth House is the place for creativity, romance, games, and children, this placement can sometimes bring blockages or challenges with the aforementioned. This is a certain amount of emotional restriction; the heart chakra is bound up or overly protected, giving those with a Fifth-House Saturn an aura of aloofness. This is far from the truth, as these people are quite warm-hearted, but shy. Whether due to childhood wounds or karmic memories, they are protecting their hearts from being hurt. With encouragement and love from family and friends, these people will blossom and express profound warmth. They need to take care of their hearts and circulation and should get plenty of fresh air and exercise. As far as creativity, these individuals might not try every hobby under the sun, but they will work at their chosen art forms with dedication and diligence. They are the ones who can master a musical instrument or understand the complexities of a camera and traditional darkroom techniques. They are also skilled at managing others in arts professions.

Uranus in the Fifth House

These could be some of the most talented children around—they are inventive, original, and creative and can bring wonderful gifts or, without proper channeling, a lot of woe to parents and teachers. They're almost too different for adults to understand. But with guidance and flexibility, their special brand of genius can be set free. As adults, these people need to learn about living within society's rules.

Neptune in the Fifth House

Here are the movie and media stars of the zodiac. They love to entertain and feel at home in show business. Sometimes a career onstage or on the big screen doesn't materialize, and they throw their sense of drama into romances, sometimes secretive and frequently passionate and idealized—all of which can bring disappointment. The heart needs to be balanced with the head. These people may also have karmic issues with loved ones that need to be played out, especially with their children. Their offspring could need special attention, which would also balance the self-centeredness left over from previous lives.

Pluto in the Fifth House

Pluto in this house gives these individuals very special skills. Children with this placement can be unusually gifted—prodigies in music, art, theater, or literature. Parents of such children should take care to nurture their gifts. If so, they could see them grow into creative geniuses. If their artistic talents are suppressed or unappreciated, however, these young people could turn to more self-destructive pursuits. They are especially curious about the opposite sex, since the Fifth House also concerns love and romance. All people with this placement should remember to use their abundant sexual energy with love, and never overpower or manipulate their lovers and mates. Adults with a Fifth-House Pluto, if they were properly encouraged as children, are abundantly creative and may even make a living from their artistic skills. Individuals with this placement are also lucky with investments and real estate speculation, but should take care to save the wealth they amass.

CHAPTER NINE

Sixth House:
We Can Work It Out

Work, work, work. Sometimes it seems like that's all the Sixth House is about, especially if a person has a grouping of planets here.

With the importance placed on one's job and career in America, the mounting pressure to produce more and more, and the way Americans now take their work home with them—not to mention the stingy vacation time we get, in contrast to the rest of the industrialized world—I think that the businesses in the United States have to reassess their priorities.

It's true. As I write this, it's summer, and it seems everyone but me is on vacation. I needed to reach someone in Holland—well, forget that. In the Netherlands they have about six weeks of vacation. France empties out in August, because everyone has a month off. Same thing in many European and Scandinavian countries. Only Japan makes its workers toil as much as we do.

Our almost obsessive work ethic must make the rest of the world wonder. But I digress.

What is so tragic is that work can be meaningful if it resonates with your soul's purpose. The point isn't to be idle (well, maybe sometimes) but to do something meaningful, something that energizes your inner being. I think this is the source of much unhappiness for many Americans, no matter what is going on in their various houses. But this is especially true for Sixth-House people.

You can pay a person with a Sixth-House Sun a zillion dollars to do some crummy job (like choosing which poor souls to lay off so the company can make more money), and something in these thoughtful folks dies. The energy of the money just doesn't resonate with them. They must serve in some way, and often they will be willing to put their noses to the grindstone in thankless positions—but not forever, and especially not when a slow-moving planet like Saturn is impacting their Sixth House.

"We fulfill the Sixth House part of our lives by finding the right work and colleagues, and by disciplining ourselves to work well," write River and Gillespie in *The Knot of Time*. "The Sixth House describes the role of work within our lives, and the need we have for work mates and colleagues as well as the importance and nature of our relationships with them."[1]

There can be problems with an emphasized Sixth House when the person overidentifies with work, so that being laid off or having to leave temporarily causes loss-of-identity issues. Or, the person can become a workaholic, committing too much to the workplace.

This rings true for my husband. With Saturn impacting his Sixth-House Gemini Sun, he has had one crisis after another at work.

With the Sun, Moon, Saturn, and Uranus in the Sixth House, Mr. Bryan is the perfect employee. He never calls in sick, is utterly punctual, and will labor endlessly, forsaking a decent meal, a union-stipulated rest, and interaction with his colleagues. He seriously needs to take a break.

This work ethic is so strong in him that he even worked his young fingers to the bone as a high school kid. When he went "on vacation" with his grandparents, his great uncle put him to work, paying him about one dollar a week to bus tables and do various kitchen chores in his fishing camp. Some vacation, huh?

He had another job, at a very young age, as a short-order cook. He was too young to drive and would pedal home on his bike, being chased by the dogs in the neighborhood because he smelled like hamburgers. Not even the dogs would give him a break!

His current job is with a good newspaper in a large northeastern city, an organization that keeps whittling down its staff, so much so that Mr. Bryan jokes that someday one per-

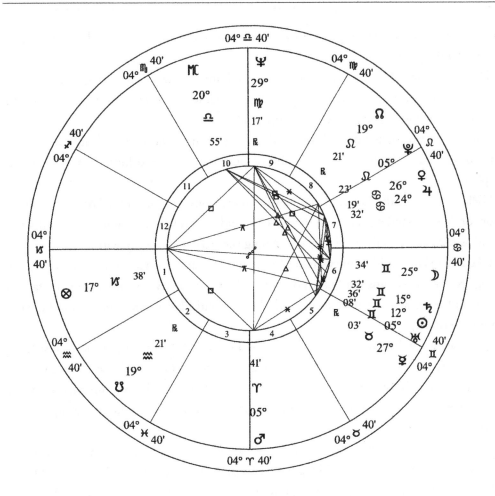

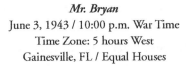

Mr. Bryan
June 3, 1943 / 10:00 p.m. War Time
Time Zone: 5 hours West
Gainesville, FL / Equal Houses

son will run the place—writing the stories, taking the pictures, answering the phones, and cleaning up the place.

They give him way too much work, though, knowing, with his strong Sixth House, that he will move heaven and earth to get things done, while his colleagues go out for chai lattés and Vietnamese food, if they show up at all.

This makes my husband, with his Sixth-House need for fairness and support for the underdogs in life, quite frustrated. This house position might also indicate a tendency to complain a lot.

Well, that's the Sixth House. Happy to work like a horse, people with a Sixth-House Sun, Moon, or Saturn—and especially all three—can't understand why everyone else doesn't work as hard as they do. And they get angry watching the slackers get away with it.

Like most people with a busy Sixth House, my husband wants to protect and help his colleagues, especially those in lesser positions. He is constantly worried about the fate of lower paid friends and the amount of work they do, and I have to remind him to be more selfish sometimes.

There are a few lessons to understand here. First of all, Sixth-House folks must learn that not everyone has as strong a work ethic as they do. Other people's priorities may be different, or they simply can't work as hard. Perhaps they have figured out that it doesn't matter anyway—who needs to be tied to the desk when we're all going to end up leaving this veil of tears?

Sixth-House people also look to their bosses to be as perfect as they are—and are wounded when a boss displays disloyalty. For those with a Sixth-House Saturn, this harks back to a need for a father figure, probably due to karmic or other issues with their own father. They idealize their bosses sometimes, whereas for most of us, the boss just isn't going to be an ideal guy or gal.

Sixth-House people look for praise, too, and are disappointed when that doesn't come. This is where they need to love themselves more, and sometimes that means unshackling themselves from a toxic situation—even if it means a cut in pay—and finding work that better feeds their souls.

A Saturn cycle or another slow-moving planet, including Uranus, impacting the Sixth House might be prodding these folks to rethink and reassess their philosophies about work. It is becoming increasingly difficult to do so, but Sixth-House people must find some kind of work that fulfills the highest vibration of "service"—something that energizes their very souls. Being a wage slave will sooner or later become intolerable.

Advocating for those with less power—perhaps as a shop steward, a consumer advocate, or a civil liberties lawyer—will bring them a feeling of satisfaction. Working with people who live in poverty will also feed their souls.

In addition, the Sixth House also rules health issues and is associated with Virgo, so exploring the mind-body connection, psychic healing, or energy work is also fulfilling to people with planets in the Sixth House.

And while efficient service in the workplace means a lot, awareness of and service to one's own health is also of great concern to the Sixth-House person. The Sixth is the house of health, diet, and exercise and is often where we look to predict what kind of illness may befall a person (and also to prevent illness). Mr. Bryan, with Gemini on the Sixth-House cusp, ruled by Mercury, is a high-strung guy, and I beg him to leave his desk once in a while and at least walk around a little. He takes the stress in his abdomen, evoking the Sixth House's connection with Virgo.

For those who love a Sixth-House person, or for the individuals themselves, consider body and energy work, such as Reiki. Sound and music therapy—concentrating on the beautiful overtones of a Tibetan prayer bowl, for example—would also be beneficial. Mindful walking, especially barefoot, works wonders. So does yoga.

If you find a lot of planets in the Sixth House, don't feel you are destined for illness or a nervous breakdown, but please pay attention to health concerns and be open to alternative methods of healing. Mostly, be aware that for people with this house placement, emotional habits and nerves wreak the most havoc.

Psychotherapy, meditation, and just plain old taking it easy are the best ways to circumvent illness.

With wisdom, finding something that resonates with the very soul will be the best curative for a life that has lost its meaning or direction. This requires some effort and soul-searching, to be sure, but who works harder than a Sixth-House person? These folks can direct this energy into healing themselves and finding meaningful work.

When the chips have been really down, my husband has found joy in his photography, playing music, or even doing housework or taking care of the garden and the birds in the backyard. Preparing for an art exhibit gives him just enough of a challenge. Interestingly, Sixth-House people thrive on challenges and are fidgety if things are too relaxed.

Most of all, Sixth-House folks need to take time for themselves. Remember, on their deathbeds, people never wish they'd spent more time in the office.

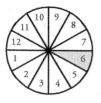 *Sixth House:* Ruled by Mercury and associated with Virgo, this is the house of work and workplace conditions, service, attitudes toward coworkers and those in lower socioeconomic groups, health, and interest in physical and mental well-being.

Planets in the Sixth House

Sun in the Sixth House

"What, me worry?" Yes, you do. Worrywarts from a young age, these folks chew and chew on ways to improve themselves, their work, their surroundings, and even their partners. They are very hard-working, loyal employees and are helpful to coworkers, especially those in lesser positions. But they can also be whiners. They really do feel that life is especially hard for them, and they air their self-pity in earnest. They try so hard to be of service that those around them want to be sympathetic. Build them up with positive affirmations, body work (such as Reiki), and praise. They need to take their vitamins and exercise to work out the mental anguish. Otherwise, their nerves can wreak havoc, especially on the digestive system.

Moon in the Sixth House

If you have this placement, watch your health, which means watch your mental health as well as physical health, because the two are closely linked with this lunar house position. Nervous disorders and worry can especially trouble the abdominal area—stomach, intestines, digestion, elimination. These people have a dedication to service and a talent for fixing things.

Mercury in the Sixth House

Computer crash? Virus coming through the "back door"? Mouse needs mending? Call Sixth-House Mercury, the original systems geeks and Dilbert-like engineers. They're geniuses with gadgetry and electronic doodads. These people are great to have around, but their love of electronics and thingamabobs—too much emphasis on the brain and mental matters—can alienate them from the heart chakra and cause them to ignore their health. Living in their heads leads to jittery nerves and psychosomatic illnesses. Remember, you can't hug a laptop.

Venus in the Sixth House

This is an interesting and offbeat placement, much like Venus in Virgo. These people make great coworkers but can be fussy and undemonstrative lovers. They want you to be as perfect as they are, but they won't let you reciprocate—you simply mustn't criticize them. They can dish it out, but they can't take it. Usually popular people in the workplace, they will lead the charge for better conditions or will blow the whistle on a scoundrel. But they need to lighten up on their spouses and lovers and get down and dirty once in a while.

Mars in the Sixth House

These folks are industrious, efficient, dynamic, and active at work. They have a tendency to become irritated, especially at minutiae and coworkers who may not be as strong or energetic. This position favors those with mechanical inclinations—this is the person who is able to put Ikea furniture together or get the car through inspection.

Jupiter in the Sixth House

People with this placement have enthusiasm for work and kinship with coworkers. They should be aware that they can give too much to their employers. As the saying goes, on their deathbeds, no one ever says, "I wish I had spent more time at the office." There might also be a tendency to overdo it in other ways, such as eating and drinking.

Saturn in the Sixth House

My husband ("Mr. Bryan") has this placement, and it's a blessing and a curse. He's about the best worker an employer could ask for, and will do the jobs no one else wants to do. At one point in his life, he was willing to shovel out chicken coops at a university agriculture department, which tickled his good-old-boy coworkers. "Looka that college boy, shovelin' chicken poop," they'd laugh. But his current employers know how strong his work ethic is, so they hand him more work than he really should have, knowing he will do anything to get it done. That's Saturn in the Sixth House. Words of wisdom would be "take a break!"

And give coworkers a break if they aren't the working machine you are, Sixth-House Saturn. My husband is always complaining about this guy or that one who sits around talking or taking a long lunch while he keeps his nose to the grindstone. Well, they figured it out. The work will be there when they get back. His former good-old-boy coworkers tried to tell my husband this a long time ago. "You might as well not hurry, because The Man will always have more work for you," they said. True, indeed.

Uranus in the Sixth House

There was this one writer where I worked who never seemed to be at his desk or even come into the building but who always turned in lengthy, elegant pieces on deadline. He was sometimes spotted coming into the building at 3 a.m. or would phone in his stories from some far-flung place. This is typical behavior for someone with Uranus in the Sixth House. These folks keep odd hours and have unorthodox ways of getting their work done, but are talented and conscientious. It was good that my colleague liked to work that way, because when he was around, he was insufferable, another common characteristic of this placement. These people can be very rude to their colleagues—but that could be due to their nerves, which often plague them.

Neptune in the Sixth House

"Chi" is sometimes defined as the life force that drives the universe and pulsates through the various energy centers in our bodies. It could also be called "prana," "presence," or "aura." Unfortunately, people with Neptune in the Sixth House have weakened chi and would do well to strengthen their energy fields through body work, such as Reiki, as well as herbal supplements and good nutrition. They are extremely sensitive, and this is a big reason why their energy fields can be compromised. They should employ a healthy dose of objectivity when it comes to dealing with people, because their innate kindness may subject them to deceit, especially in the workplace.

Pluto in the Sixth House

Put the explosive energy of Pluto in the house of service and work, and kapow—these are the people who do the deep, dark dirty work no one else wants to do, like the folks who clean up nuclear accidents. Because of an inferiority complex, they grumble about doing the "grunt" work and sometimes feel it is their destiny. They also have the strength to help others through crises, sometimes to their own detriment, because they can work themselves into illness. Thorough and fair, with a combination of intuitive and analytical abilities, these people make excellent psychologists.

---

1. Lindsay River and Sally Gillespie, *The Knot of Time* (New York: Harper & Row, 1987), p. 235.

CHAPTER TEN

Seventh House:
It Takes Two

Caesar and Cleopatra. Napoleon and Josephine. Nicholas and Alexandra. Victoria and Albert. John and Yoko. John and Paul. Ronnie and Nancy. Sid and Nancy.

Even more so than single people in history, couples seem to jump out at us. I could go on and on with the list of twosomes, who together made history of some kind when, alone, they might have been forgotten.

This is the essence of the Seventh House—which has to do with marriage, partnerships, and joint ventures. Whether it is loaded with planets or empty, this house gives clues to how we will interact with others, especially those with whom we have a more intimate relationship.

It is the natural place for the sign of Libra, which is associated with the law and the scales of justice. The Seventh House also resonates with legal matters, negotiations, and contracts—manmade things that we put together to codify how we will conduct ourselves in regard to others.

In primitive times, such pieces of paper did not exist. Today, people frequently complain that there are too many lawyers and you can be sued for almost anything. We lament that's there's too much litigation, that in the past there never was the need for so many rules of behavior—all you needed was a person's word or a handshake to forge a deal. Perhaps the Libran values of fairness and equality have somehow disintegrated in our "me first" culture and competitive capitalist society, where the philosophy abounds that the "one who dies with the most toys wins."

The kind of idealism that would require only a handshake is something people with Neptune in the Seventh House (or Pisces on the cusp of the Seventh House) might espouse. Sadly, their idealism could be shattered when such ideals are crushed, but this might be a lesson these people have to learn in midlife, or over the course of this incarnation.

Another side of the Seventh House is how the people you meet experience or react to you. It has to do with interaction and confrontations and, sometimes, open enemies (as opposed to the Twelfth House, which has to do with hidden enemies).

The Seventh House also governs how and where we draw strength from other people. "The purpose of the seventh house is to bring about greater self-awareness through relating to what we experience as being outside of ourselves—it has to do with what psychologists call 'projection,'" write River and Gillespie in *The Knot of Time*.[1]

The Seventh House is also where the Descendant is located. As we learned from the discussion of the Descendant in chapter 2, if a person hasn't fully matured or individuated, and she's still in the process of "filling in the gaps" of her personality and strengths, she could be drawn to someone who does this for her. That's the layperson's explanation of the psychological phenomenon of projection.

Interestingly, a person with an incomplete personality could also easily fall in with someone who reminds her of unacknowledged weaknesses.

For example, the person with the Neptunian or Piscean Seventh House would project idealism, a love of fantasy and romance, perhaps a gentle or shy personality, and maybe a tendency toward escapism. She would be attracted to a very different kind of person, almost her opposite, one who has it together and relishes being in the world, someone with a firm—even cynical—grip on reality. This would be the masculine, worldly "yang" to Seventh-House Neptune's ethereal, feminine "yin."

Western culture and mythology are filled with tales of the fair maiden in need of rescuing. There is usually an archetypal knight out there, a practical, feet-on-the-ground man who needs just the opposite of himself—a dreamy, romantic woman to remind him of the softer, lovelier things in the world.

The problem is, that kind of a story is a fairy tale. We can't find everything we lack in another person.

Psychologists say that's mostly what falling in love is about—seeing the personality traits in another person that we lack in ourselves. What we hope to work toward—and this may take a lifetime or many lifetimes—is finding the missing pieces within ourselves.

Referring to *The Knot of Time* again, River and Gillespie write that through the Seventh House "we can tell what qualities the person has repressed and discarded in herself. When the descending sign attracts, it is because we project our own undeveloped positive traits, often compulsively falling in love with our 'opposite' or complement."[2]

I keep mentioning Seventh-House Neptune because a client of mine with this placement has an interesting but tragic love life. Through her kindness and acceptance of people from all walks of life (and a tendency to be in love with love and to need to feel needed), she is repeatedly attracted to helpless men.

It's as though she keeps finding little lost kittens on her doorstep, instead of real men. Their romantic qualities appeal to her at first, and their need for her love makes her feel needed. But disaster has struck again and again when the neediness turns into possessiveness and outright mooching. They seem to reject the nine-to-five working world (she loves artists and musicians), and eventually they sponge off of her.

The unacknowledged part of our shadow soul pops up to remind us it's there, often in the guise of folks at work we just can't seem to get along with, dysfunctional intimate relationships, and even rude people who might be waiting on us at the bank or a restaurant.

This is true with my client's love life. The men in her life and their neediness both attract and repel her. Perhaps she is too independent and needs to learn to ask for help more often. Or maybe she was needy in a previous life and is balancing out this pattern, learning to draw boundaries.

Whereas a person with a busy Twelfth House might retreat into the solitary life of an artist or monk, those with an activated Seventh House need others to help them work out their own issues. They keep trying to make relationships work, sometimes to the detriment of their own self-growth. They tamp down their own needs and personalities or try to mirror their partners in order to please them.

Since the Seventh House has to do with Libra, a bit of the Libran balance needs to be utilized here. Where do the needs of your partner or your family end, and where do your needs begin? If there are challenging aspects to the Seventh House, you must learn how to balance your needs with those of others around you, especially a significant other.

Relationship crises, especially those that recur, are often signals that we have not thought through our priorities. Or, in midlife, if planets are transiting the Seventh House, it may be time to look inward to find the gaps in our personalities—the traits we haven't addressed, good and bad—and better understand them. It's part of learning to love ourselves.

Perhaps through psychotherapy, journaling, or art therapy (Venus rules the Seventh House, so Seventh-House folks often have artistic leanings) we can become more familiar with our inner partner. Although partnership and friendship are always wonderful, doing the work on yourself is ultimately necessary to become a whole person. When all of the blank spaces have been filled in, and a person glows with inner strength, even the loneliest Seventh-House soul can't help but attract others. But you have to do the work first.

I wonder if Martha Stewart will reassess her relationship priorities now that the insider-trading scandal is behind her. Her Saturn in the Seventh House has many implications concerning marriage. The disastrous divorce she and her husband went through is common knowledge. She has Mars in Aries, which signifies haste, so I suspect she might have rushed into the marriage, either through youthful infatuation or through financial or social pressures. Saturn in this placement can indicate people who marry too young and hang in there when there's no more love left in the relationship. Then it's apt to end in an unhappy way. Or, with Saturn, the partner may be older or have a serious nature that restricts the spontaneity of the partnership. It's not a good placement for a lighthearted, romantic marriage. However, it could mean the marriage will begin with problems but become lighter as the years pass.

I discovered another celebrity chart with a lively Seventh House, and it's a lighter story—but one that is rife with partnership issues. It's Warren Beatty's chart.

A notorious womanizer, his affections have been shared with a legion of females in Hollywood and beyond. Various tallies include Madonna, Diane Keaton, Liv Ullmann, Julie Christie, Michelle Phillips, Joan Collins, Vanessa Redgrave, Brigitte Bardot, and on and on. To his credit, he doesn't discuss his love life with the media.

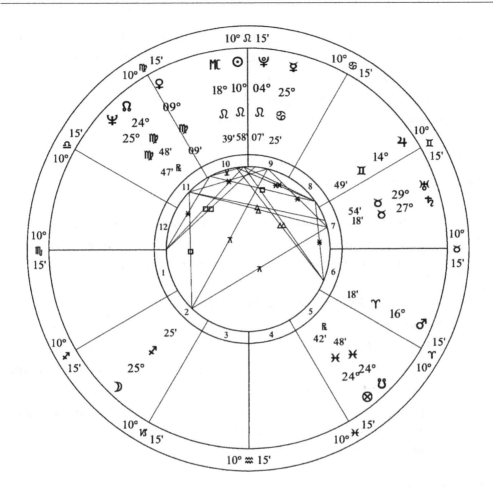

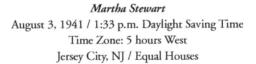

Martha Stewart
August 3, 1941 / 1:33 p.m. Daylight Saving Time
Time Zone: 5 hours West
Jersey City, NJ / Equal Houses

At age fifty-six, Beatty married Annette Bening, and their first child was born shortly after—daughter Kathlyn. As a family man, he and Bening added three more children in the following few years.

Was there a missing element to his personality that he found in Bening? Did all those other women he dated somehow satisfy what was lacking in himself? Growing up with a stern father and a domineering stage mother,[3] he may not have fully related to himself without a woman either telling him what to do or reflecting his ego back to him.

These are all projection issues, and the very heart of the Seventh House's lessons.

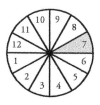

Seventh House: Associated with Libra and governed by Venus, the Seventh House has to do with group awareness and cooperative relationships and partnerships, such as marriages or business alliances.

Planets in the Seventh House

Sun in the Seventh House

These folks are some of the best friends, partners, spouses, and lovers of all the Sun placements in the houses. Solitude bugs them—they really need to be with others, especially one special person. Their desire for compatibility is so strong that they may submerge their own needs and personality. Or they may insist on "ruling the roost" in a marriage or partnership, sometimes to its detriment. This placement is a clue that there are karmic issues of equality that need to be resolved.

Moon in the Seventh House

These chameleons have the ability to partner with a variety of folks. If you have this placement, be careful not to sweep your own personality under the rug in order to fit in. These people may be obsessed with popularity, because they have a strong need to be with other people, one special person in particular.

Mercury in the Seventh House

If you are married to someone with a Seventh-House Mercury, you'll need to brush up on your witty rapport and communications skills. Spouses, partners, and close friends also should be patient if these folks can't seem to tear loose from CNN. They need to stay in touch with the national and international news and like for their partners to be up on

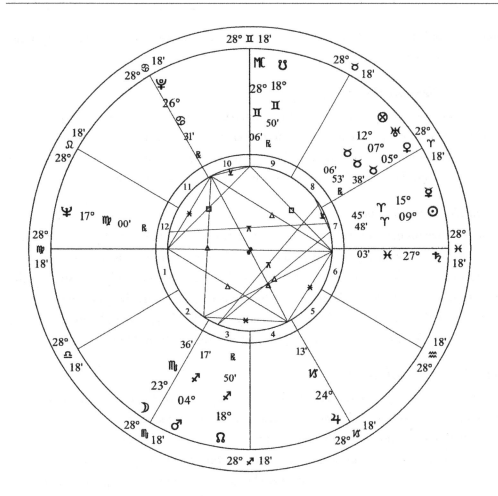

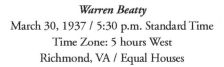

Warren Beatty
March 30, 1937 / 5:30 p.m. Standard Time
Time Zone: 5 hours West
Richmond, VA / Equal Houses

things too—and that means the world out there. They also like their partners and spouses to be good debaters.

Venus in the Seventh House

This placement generally indicates a happy marriage and successful partnerships, unless aspected poorly. These people are fortunate in that the spouse is usually well-off or gifted in some way, including in appearance. They are friendly and loving, but may be a bit too trusting. They could expect others to be equally enlightened and loving.

Mars in the Seventh House

If there are challenging aspects in the chart, there is karma to deal with here—these individuals have been too arrogant in previous lives. They are here in this incarnation, with this placement, to balance the residue of a "me first" attitude. So there might be strife in the partnership, or it might seem like they are bending over backwards, always giving in to the other person. Otherwise, there will be much energy employed in running a house that hums. A person with a Seventh-House Mars needs to be the boss at the old homestead.

Jupiter in the Seventh House

Because of their optimism and excellent character judgment, these people will attract positive opportunities—beneficial business colleagues, social contacts, and marriage partners. A Seventh-House Jupiter could indicate a person who will marry more than once, or will marry someone who has been wed before. For a woman with this placement, marriage might bring an older male partner, someone who is established in the religious or academic community. A Seventh-House Jupiter brings a sense of justice, so these individuals will be certain to treat others fairly. If poorly aspected, they might be too optimistic or naïve about relationships and could be taken advantage of.

Saturn in the Seventh House

Saturn in this house indicates that marriage, friendship, and partnerships have been painful in previous lives, and the person is hesitant to connect. Open communication is a way to master challenges in relationships, marriage, and business partnerships. If you have this placement and feel somewhat stifled or discouraged from speaking the truth, gather your courage and let it rip. Even if your partner argues or disagrees, your point of view will be out there. Love and marriage might feel painful sometimes to those with a Seventh-House Saturn, and they might want to run away, seeking solace in solitude. They need to remember that partnerships are always in flux. There will be high and low points, but with patience and faith, individuals with this placement will find the happy center point and make peace with their loved ones, eventually creating mature and meaningful relationships.

Uranus in the Seventh House

Uranus in the Seventh House indicates individuals whose lives are filled with unusual people—some beneficial, some not. Partnerships are intriguing and chock full of surprises. People with a Seventh-House Uranus sometimes feel misunderstood, because they stand somewhat apart from the mainstream. Marriage takes work because these folks love their independence, or they could attract a free-spirited partner who doesn't want to be restricted. This placement reminds me of my friend John, who had acquaintances from all walks of life, literally saints and sinners. He had mentors setting him up in the coffee business, and professors, authors, artists, and even a Zen Buddhist monk would come to his coffee shop, sit and chat, invite him for meals, give him wonderful gifts, and lend him money. Unfortunately, one of the more unsavory friends gave him something else—drugs.

Neptune in the Seventh House

Neptune in this house indicates karma having to do with partnerships or marriage, so these people may feel like they are working extra hard to appease a significant other who is not reciprocating. If you have this placement, think of it as exercise, like working out—there is pain, but it's good pain, which will lead to strength. It's the same with this kind of karma. Try to reflect on the deeper meaning and long-term effect that understanding this circumstance will have on the soul's education. The significant other may have real talent in the arts, and folks with this placement can better connect with the partner through appreciating his or her talents.

Pluto in the Seventh House

Folks with a Seventh-House Pluto can be either diplomatic or argumentative, depending on other aspects and planetary placements. They seem to move among a variety of people and may find it hard to settle down in a harmonious relationship with one person. They need to use wisdom in choosing a life or business partner, because Pluto—the slowest-moving heavenly body—creates very long-lasting relationships, even if the individual wishes to extract himself. With this placement, there could be natural talent in law, since these individuals have the ability to see both sides of a situation objectively. A career as a mediator or in corporate law could be especially successful.

1. Lindsay River and Sally Gillespie, *The Knot of Time* (New York: Harper & Row, 1987), p. 236.

2. Ibid.

3. Lois Rodden, "Newsmaker's Chart for Warren Beatty," *AstroDatabank*, http://www.astrodatabank.com/ NM/BeattyWarrenPRT.htm.

CHAPTER ELEVEN

Eighth House:
Sex, Death, and Detective Work

One of the signs of civilization's portending demise is this trend to emblazon titillating slogans on the posterior. You know, those shorts and sweatpants that say "hot stuff" or "can't touch this." When the little girls' departments in family-oriented stores are filled with midriff tops that say "juicy" on crucial areas of the body, there's something really wrong with America's attitude toward sex. It's a trend that I just can't seem to warm up to, but maybe I'm getting old—a leftover from the women's liberation movement. I think women should, instead, wear magnificent hats that say "I'm really smart" or "Goddess upstairs" or "look at my breasts and I'll punch you."

A person with planets in the Eighth House, or Scorpio on the Eighth-House cusp, would probably agree. Ruled by Pluto and the natural place for Scorpio, the Eighth House wants us to have respect for sex. "Your ad here" on the buttocks is more childlike, like the impulsive Fifth House–approach to sex. "Jump on it!" the Fifth House says.

I think of Aldous Huxley's 1932 novel *Brave New World*, which foresaw test-tube babies, among other contemporary scientific breakthroughs. In the book, people are no longer born, but "decanted" in a laboratory. So sexuality isn't for procreation; it's purely recreational. The characters don't have loving, long-term relationships, but just a series of empty one-night stands, without passion or meaning.

This kind of sexuality is the opposite of the essence of the Eighth House, and so is this cheapening trend of advertising one's "hotness."

The Eighth House resonates with mature, meaningful sexuality. Sex is a beautiful thing—ancient, mysterious, primal—and the Eighth-House essence of sexuality is about connection, divinity, and mystery.

Journeying around the wheel of the houses, we are well above the horizon at the Eighth House, and the planets placed in the Eighth and subsequent houses denote gaining wisdom beyond mere survival consciousness. The Eighth House in particular has to do with complex subject matters—death, psychic phenomena, and also "other people's money," like investments and communal funds, such as taxes. But most of all, the Eighth House marks a person's attitude toward sexuality.

For those who study healing and the chakras, the reproductive organs and genitals are associated with the second chakra. The sign of Scorpio is also linked to this part of the body, and so the second chakra naturally connects with the Eighth House.

This is one of the most primal areas of the body, one of the places where we evolved beyond the other primates. We learned that genitals and reproductive organs are necessary for the very continuation of the species as well as the ecstasy from the act of creating new life. The discovery that mating could take place face to face was not only a giant step in the evolution of mating and sociology but a leap forward in human consciousness. Now sex wasn't merely a biological act to satisfy the man's various "itches" and to add to the tribe's ranks.

When humans evolved enough to make love face to face, the soul and the essence of sexuality evolved as well. (Interestingly, dolphins also make love face to face.) It is not only the genitals that come together—all the chakras are connected. The physical act of sex brings energy up through the lower chakras, through the heart, throat, and eyes, and—in the moment of ecstasy—through the crown and outward into the ethers. We experience a brief moment when we shed our egos and touch the Universal Source—satori, nirvana, the Goddess. Oneness.

A person with planets emphasized in the Eighth House, or Scorpio on the Eighth-House cusp, would be inclined to understand the power of sexuality and would be interested in the deeper meaning of sex.

On the other hand, challenging aspects to planets in the Eighth House may make the native preoccupied with some of the baser forms of sexual exploitation, as we have seen more and more in this age of high technology. Child pornography, violence, and even ritualistic murder can be lived vicariously through the Internet or visual recordings.

Happily, those with challenges to the Eighth House are also able to dig deep and use their profound insights to handle thorny issues, such as sexual addictions or quirks.

The Eighth House also reminds us of our mortality. If the Sun is here in a person's chart, it means the person was born late in the afternoon, metaphorically, as the light was dying and the secretive night was descending.

Therefore, the Eighth House also has to do with death. However, it doesn't mean you should become obsessed with the Grim Reaper if you have many planets in the Eighth House of your natal chart or are experiencing a slow-moving planet like Saturn transiting your Eighth House.

If you are reading this book, it is likely that you are a student of the mysteries and metaphors associated with death. When I write about and counsel people using the tarot, I teach that the Death card is rife with esoteric connotations—it rarely means "literal death." It could indicate the death of a bad habit, the end of a cycle or relationship, the metamorphosis from one stage of life to the next. It's the same with an emphasis on the Eighth House, which suggests a time of day when the Earth moves on its axis toward the mysterious evening—it's the end of the day to some but just the beginning for others. As the sun sets in this part of the world, a new day is dawning on the other side.

Or, think of the seasons, when the darkest, shortest day of the year—the winter solstice—means chills, bundling up, and chasing away the darkness with candles, songs, and celebration. These are very primitive ways that our culture learned to honor the darkness—the death of the light—and look forward to the return of the sun. Some thought that if they made enough noise and lit enough fires, the gods who swallowed the sun would spit it out and the light would return. It must have worked for them. After all, the days begin to get longer after the solstice.

Edgar Cayce was one man with his Sun in the Eighth House who understood that eternal light follows darkness. In fact, he disputed that we ever really die at all. The "Sleeping Prophet" planted the seeds for many people interested in karma and reincarnation, although

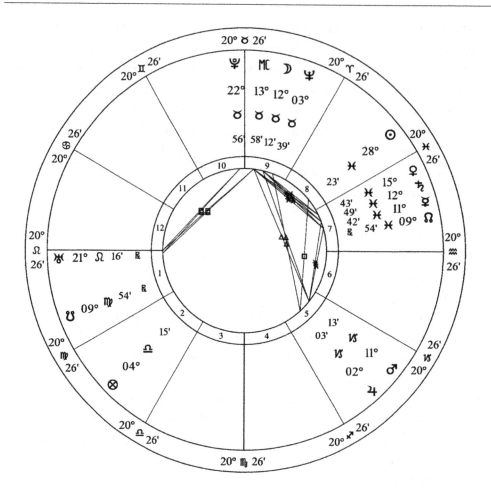

Edgar Cayce
March 18, 1877 / 3:00 p.m. Local Mean Time
Time Zone: 0 hours West
Hopkinsville, KY / Equal Houses

he was born into a strict Protestant family, in Hopkinsville, Kentucky—a most unlikely place for a seer and "godfather" of the New Age movement.[1]

Even in childhood, he claims to have had visitations and communications with angels and the etheric realms. Other children (and adults) thought he was odd, but he remained steadfast in his beliefs and faith.

Later in life, thousands of people came to Cayce for readings to help them understand the most profound, difficult questions humans have asked for millennia—especially about death. With his Sun in the Eighth House, perhaps Cayce incarnated to help people address these issues. His soul may have chosen to "land" in relatively tolerant, multicultural America so that his information could be disseminated without censorship. Imagine, on the other hand, someone like Edgar Cayce trying to communicate his knowledge in an impoverished country with a rigid, fundamentalist culture.

Even several decades after Cayce's passing, the appreciation of all these spiritual and metaphysical matters—many of which resonate with the Eighth House—goes on at the Association for Research and Enlightenment (A.R.E.) in Virginia Beach, Virginia.

It was Gina Cerminara's book about Cayce, *Many Mansions*, that gave me faith in the eternal life of the soul, much more so than a dozen years of Catholic education. It made me lose the fear of death and judgment that so many organized religions place deep inside the minds and hearts of their adherents.

Years after discovering *Many Mansions* and after sundry visits to the A.R.E. and a lot of independent study (both academic study and soul searching), I know in my heart that physical death is not the end of the soul's journey. Don't ask me why and how I know. It's a difficult standpoint to defend with empirical evidence. I just know, or perhaps *believe*, that there's more to life than what is merely on the surface, comprehended through the senses.

Perhaps those with planets in the Eighth House are nodding in agreement and understanding.

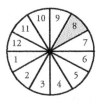 *Eighth House:* The natural house for Scorpio and governed by Pluto, the Eighth House has to do with sex, death, the mysteries of life, investments, and other people's money.

Planets in the Eighth House

Sun in the Eighth House

The Eighth House is tied in with Scorpio and Pluto, so there is mysterious, volcanic energy when the Sun is placed here. These natives have a natural inclination toward the occult and maybe some genuine psychic abilities. A magnetic, outwardly calm demeanor masks strong emotions. They may have a karmic need to regenerate themselves, perhaps by overcoming an egotistical or manipulative personality, the residue of previous lives.

Moon in the Eighth House

These individuals can be overly sensitive or could be partnered with someone who is overly sensitive, to the point of it being problematic. However, this hypersensitivity can be developed into psychic ability as well as financial acumen. This is a placement for a good psychologist.

Mercury in the Eighth House

I wonder if Detective Munch on *Law & Order: Special Victims Unit* has this placement? The character (played by Richard Belzer) always gets into the psychological reasons the "perps" have done what they've done, usually something connected with childhood, which the much-wounded Munch can relate to. People with an Eighth-House Mercury are excellent detectives, researchers, and analysts. But, also like Munch, they can be neurotics, worrywarts, and sometimes gossips.

Venus in the Eighth House

This is a lucky placement, with money and possessions coming through inheritances. Or, the fortune may come through legacies of the marriage partner, through wealthy in-laws and extended family members of the spouse. Individuals with this placement have strong convictions and opinions—don't contradict them—and will attract power, or will be the power behind the throne. They enjoy unique friends as well as unusual pleasures. Since Venus likes to take it easy, these individuals could be too casual with their inheritances, going through money faster than most. A practical partner with a level-headed Sun or Moon sign will balance out this tendency. Or, the extravagance of Eighth-House Venus could be balanced by these individuals having their own Sun, Moon or other planets in an earth sign.

Mars in the Eighth House

Whether it's bird watching, playing the stock market, or studying voodoo, these folks will enthusiastically plumb the depths of any matter that piques their curiosity. This is the house of "other people's money," and if poorly aspected, there could be difficulties with a partner's money—perhaps disentangling the financial knots for a partner who has run up too much debt. On the other hand, partnerships and marriage could bring financial gains.

Jupiter in the Eighth House

These folks might look forward to a nice inheritance, as there is good fortune in things ruled by the Eighth House, including grants, gifts, and bequests. Their positive attitude, combined with natural psychic abilities, can be channeled into humanitarian or spiritual work, often helping to raise other people's consciousness.

Saturn in the Eighth House

Like monks, these individuals may deny themselves the pleasures of life, believing too strongly that service and suffering will lead to higher consciousness. That belief should be taken with a grain of salt. We are placed on the Earth plane to learn, certainly, but the world is a bountiful place filled with beauty, and we can deny the glory of the Source if we turn our backs on this gift. The Egyptians weighed an honored person's heart upon death, and if the heart was heavy, it was said that the person would have to return to Earth to "lose some weight." If you find Saturn in this position, use your considerable self-discipline to consciously bring joy into your life and balance out the tendency toward negativity. Lighten up!

Uranus in the Eighth House

This position could indicate a problem with temper—little volcanic eruptions of anger that occur at unpredictable times. A person with this placement would be advised to step back from the anger and, especially, to avoid using machinery (such as a car) when the blood is boiling. This explosive energy can be channeled into metaphysics, the occult, and psychic phenomena. One way to utilize this power is to explore the higher vibrational aspects of sexuality, perhaps through tantric yoga or by creating a ritualistic quality of love-making with a partner.

Neptune in the Eighth House

Here is a person with strong skills in metaphysics, someone whose connection with the etheric realm is just below waking consciousness. This placement indicates a powerful seer, someone who can turn his or her intuitive talents into a profession, but only if the skills will be used to better the human race. Becoming a charlatan or using black magic to gain personal power or material wealth will lead to failure—and bad karma.

Pluto in the Eighth House

Pluto feels like it is "home" here, so all of its positive traits will shine in this placement. These people are intuitive, with psychic abilities and an inner strength that surpasses that of individuals with a different placement of Pluto. These individuals could have good financial acumen, especially in telling others how to invest their money, or they could experience financial woes. Money comes through partnerships or inheritance.

---

1. Edgar Cayce, *My Life as a Seer: The Lost Memoirs*, compiled and edited by A. Robert Smith (New York: St. Martin's Press, 1999).

CHAPTER TWELVE

Ninth House: River Deep, Mountain High

"Imagination is more important than knowledge."
—Albert Einstein[1]

That quote may ring false to a creative person who struggles to make a living in the arts while the connect-the-dot-type engineers in the family watch their stock portfolios grow, buy sailboats, and retire when they're fifty.

Sometimes it's tough to take for those of us who have more imagination than scientific or mathematical skills, especially in the United States, which is a technology-driven country that worships empirical "knowledge."

Of course, Einstein, who made a name for himself crunching numbers and formulating theorems, didn't mean we should all sit around and navel-gaze. What made Einstein a genius was that he combined the empirical, mathematical knowledge he was schooled in with his imagination—fired by Jupiter in the Ninth House, with Aquarius on the cusp.

His quote captures succinctly the essence of Ninth-House wisdom.

The imagination he speaks of is the ability to understand and tune in to "Great Understanding" as opposed to "Little Understanding." In their book *The Tao of Photography*, Philippe L. Gross and S. I. Shapiro contrast these two kinds of knowledge. "Little Understanding represents the frame of mind concentrated on techniques, set goals (and) . . . rules . . . whereas Great Understanding . . . corresponds to the ability to respond holistically and spontaneously. Although the ability to discriminate [author's note: which I would connect with Mercury and the Third House] is beneficial for survival purposes, it can easily become an autonomous mental reflex for responding to all situations. When this happens, Great Understanding is lost: openness, receptivity, and holistic perception and understanding are repressed."[2]

The natural house for Sagittarius and ruled by Jupiter, the Ninth House represents the ability to see the big picture, to understand broader concepts in living one's life. With the Ninth House, we are near the apex of the horoscope wheel. Symbolically, we are not children anymore. It's time to think about larger issues, some of which have been presented in the Seventh and Eighth Houses—such as learning to get along with a partner, the deeper meaning of sexuality and connectedness, and death and rebirth.

The Ninth House is opposite the Third House, and it's interesting to contrast the two.

The Third House is where we gather information about our immediate environment— usually in childhood, around our neighborhood, in the home of our family of origin, or in elementary school. What kind of "knowledge" do we gather in this early stage of our lives? Usually it's the ABCs or the three Rs—some kind of rote learning, fundamental skills that allow us to make our way in the world as we grow up.

With the Ninth House—which also has a connection to higher education—things like spelling and the multiplication tables are well in place, and it's time to think about more abstract concepts.

"Knowing implies a proven fact, such as man needed oxygen to breathe," writes Myrna Lofthus in *A Spiritual Approach to Astrology*.[3] "'Understanding' comes when we have acquired wisdom through our associations with other people. The complex nature of 'understanding' and of the search for the meaning of life leads us along many pathways."

That's why foreign travel, higher education, religion, and philosophy are also associated with the Ninth House. Jupiter, the largest planet in the solar system, which has its natural home in the Ninth House, has to do with expansion. Travel, education, and such are all things that help us "expand" ourselves. We reach beyond the limitations placed on us by our family of origin, the things we learned as a child. When we expand and reach out to the world at large, we mature, we grow out of the small-mindedness children sometimes show on the playground when they're being petty. Unfortunately, some adults don't wish to acknowledge that there are other kinds of people and cultures out there, or they look down on different ways of life—or fear them. These nonexpansive people stay grooved into habits they needed to grow out of long ago, or they adhere to rules that restrict the imagination.

In contrast, when we honor and become fired up by the kind of growth offered in the Ninth House, we're open to possibilities, willing to explore, go with the flow, and perhaps discover something "out there" that changes our lives profoundly. If we are closed off to this sense of wonder and too concerned with minutiae, we may miss the opportunity for a higher education of the soul.

I can cite one clear example where I—willing to be on the vanguard of philosophical ideas—bumped up against a young boss whose mind was not flexible enough to grasp a concept I was trying to present, because he was too hung up on the "small-mindedness" of a dictionary definition.

We argued about Walt Whitman's *Leaves of Grass*. Old Uncle Walt was trying to say that all things in nature, no matter how small and insignificant, are wondrous, that even a single blade of grass is a work of art. To Whitman, even a tiny ant (which he called a "pismire," in his Victorian vocabulary) is a marvelous thing, with its tenacity and strength.

My colleague had never heard of the word pismire and found some bogus definition that he claimed had something to do with a bodily function we couldn't mention in the paper. He wanted to *paraphrase Walt Whitman's writing*—even after I showed him the poem and explained the context to him: that an ant is part of the interconnectedness of the universe. But his mentality was all blocked up in facts, Third-House stuff, and Little Understanding. Too bad he couldn't break down those concrete walls and imagine what Whitman was trying to say. The good news is that we ran Whitman's stanza, and nobody wrote to the editor in outrage because we mentioned a pismire.

The same mental inflexibility happens with religion. Dogma, a too-literal interpretation of written words—like twisting the Bible or the Koran to justify atrocities committed against other human beings—replaces a heart-and-soul-centered connection with Spirit. Sometimes

Saturn in the Ninth House, or challenging aspects to planets there, can trigger this kind of fanaticism.

Fortunately, planets in the Ninth House usually indicate a philosophical, Jovian positivity that makes us curious about what lies beyond the boundaries of our comfort zones. We listen more actively to what the other guy is saying, especially if he is saying it with a foreign accent. The Ninth House loves anything foreign.

The late Timothy Leary had a busy Ninth House. His early career was marked by conformity to tradition. He was a professor of psychology at Harvard, most likely toeing the Ivy League code of behavior until he accidentally ingested a mind-altering drug, caught a whiff of the counterculture, and led the charge to tune in, turn on, and drop out.

Now, granted, Timothy Leary went off the rails with the LSD trips (Neptune in the Ninth can cloud good judgment), but his Ninth-House heart (Leo on the cusp) was in the right place. Riding the Zeitgeist of the time, he encouraged a generation and stragglers left over from earlier social revolutions to question various aspects of the Establishment—patriarchal academia, the United States government, the military-industrial complex, and outdated social mores—all of which needed to be given a heart-centered overhaul. We could use another one today, come to think of it.

Leary was also on the leading edge of the human potentiality movement, encouraging folks to think about breaking down the "box" of normal consciousness that allows us to get by in the world, put food on the table, and hold a job, but is somewhat bereft of miracles.

Like others with planets in the Ninth House, Leary got people to understand that there is more to life than just surviving this incarnation—there is the potential for everyday miracles, if we are just open to them.

In foreshadowing many of the best things the New Age movement talks about, Leary proposed that we could shape our own reality by reframing our attitudes and consciousness, "mapping" our future with our imagination and intentions, much as author Shakti Gawain and others have discussed with the concept of creative visualization. Many of these ideas are connected with non-Western philosophies brought to the mainstream during the sixties by guys like Leary, poet Allen Ginsberg, author Ken Kesey, and any number of visionary musicians, artists, and thinkers from that era.

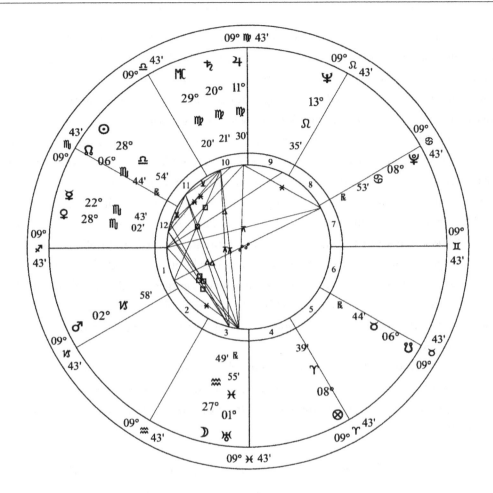

Timothy Leary
October 22, 1920 / 10:45 a.m. Daylight Saving Time
Time Zone: 5 hours West
Springfield, MA / Equal Houses

We may have swung too far in a self-destructive direction back then, and I think we have swung back in a conservative direction now. But thankfully, some of the best, most expansive Ninth-House-oriented ideas from that era live on and thrive.

You can study transpersonal psychology, human potentiality, consciousness raising, Eastern religions, philosophy, meditation, body and energy work, and even astrology and tarot at your community college or local yoga center. These subjects are now part of our popular culture—and we need all the positive Ninth-House knowledge we can get to balance the ignorance, chaos, and violence that seem to be growing by the week.

Perhaps the best way to summarize the expansive essence of the Ninth House comes from Marianne Williamson, author of *A Return to Love: Reflections on the Principles of A Course in Miracles* and international lecturer on spiritual, personal, and political issues. In one of her most famous passages, she writes: "It is our light, not our darkness, that most frightens us. We ask ourselves, Who am I to be brilliant, gorgeous, talented, fabulous? Actually, who are you *not* to be? You are a child of God. Your playing small doesn't serve the world. There is nothing enlightened about shrinking so that other people won't feel insecure around you.

"We were born to manifest the glory of God that is within us. It is not just in some of us; it is in everyone. And as we let our own light shine, we unconsciously give other people permission to do the same. As we are liberated from our own fear, our presence automatically liberates others."[4]

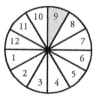 *Ninth House:* The natural house of Sagittarius and governed by Jupiter, the Ninth House is associated with higher education, religion, philosophy, ideals, foreign travel, and foreign cultures.

Planets in the Ninth House

Sun in the Ninth House

Here is the home of the Old Philosopher. This placement makes for an idealistic, expansive, progressive-minded person, in love with foreign travel and with a talent for languages. If there are challenging aspects, this could indicate the flip side of liberalism and give the person a dogmatic, skeptical mien.

Moon in the Ninth House

Which now-defunct airline used to have the slogan "We love to fly and it shows?" This describes the Ninth-House Moon. These people need to travel, study, and be occupied in a variety of expansive experiences. Thus, there may be a lack of satisfaction with a more humdrum life. These folks make great teachers, especially if it's a subject they love. They have good precognitive abilities and interesting dreams, which they might be advised to pay attention to for psychic clues.

Mercury in the Ninth House

With this placement we find teachers, preachers, and public speakers. These people have the ability to communicate their many ideas—usually on the philosophical side—to many people, in a positive, uplifting, intellectual yet accessible way. They love to travel, and it serves them well, as they are able to bring their experiences home and share them with others. These folks would be great geography teachers, but do they still teach geography in school?

Venus in the Ninth House

This is an excellent placement for an ambassador, because not only do these people love to travel, but they also have an appreciation for foreign cultures and the ability to bring different kinds of people together. With an affinity for the arts, here is the quintessential American in Paris, at the café, ordering *un vin rouge, s'il vous plait*.

Mars in the Ninth House

This is a good placement for Mars, although the fiery nature of the planet combined with Ninth-House issues such as religion and philosophy could also make these folks pompous or religious fanatics, if poorly aspected. They are restless, need freedom, and love to travel. They have strong convictions, which they will fight for.

Jupiter in the Ninth House

Jupiter is at home here in the Ninth, and shines with enthusiasm, compassion, and foresight. This placement also brings intuitive talents. These people love to travel and interact with folks they meet abroad, and such people and places bring enrichment to their lives.

Saturn in the Ninth House

This is an interesting placement, because it makes for serious, religious, conservative little boys and girls who, with education and enlightenment, become more tolerant and expansive as they grow older. (With most people, it's usually the other way around). All the Ninth-House things—philosophy, higher education, religion, foreign travel—are "weighted down" by Saturn. For example, these folks may not have the chance to go to college or may have to delay foreign travel until later in life. They are wise and conscientious, however, and make good teachers.

Uranus in the Ninth House

The house where Uranus shows up in a person's chart indicates a tendency toward erratic, sudden circumstances and unusual approaches. Since the Ninth House has to do with philosophy, religion, higher education, travel abroad, and all things foreign, this placement could indicate journeys that may come up suddenly, or an unusual, radical approach toward one's belief system. There is also a real possibility of psychic ability, especially through interpreting one's dreams.

Neptune in the Ninth House

My husband has this placement. The strength of his inner life as well as his ability to trust his intuition balance out his loaded Sixth House with four planets in Gemini. Studying mystical pursuits and Eastern philosophy has helped to quiet his "monkey mind." His knowledge gives him beautiful depth, which has also helped us through troubled times, understanding various soul lessons and knowing that, as we used to say in the sixties, "there are no accidents . . . everything happens for a reason." This kind of deeper wisdom is a hallmark of Ninth-House Neptune.

Pluto in the Ninth House

These folks are often trailblazers, with liberal, philosophical ideals, or they could be religious fanatics. They have a great desire to travel and to study, particularly religion, philosophy, and metaphysics, and they could have some intuitive talents, especially in dream work. They need to watch out for the tendency to eat, drink, or party too much. Self-indulgence or substance abuse will numb their natural psychic abilities.

1. Common attribution to Einstein, especially around Princeton, New Jersey, where Einstein lived and studied. It can be seen on bumper stickers, posters, and T-shirts.

2. Philippe L. Gross and S. I. Shapiro, *The Tao of Photography* (Berkeley, CA: Ten Speed Press, 2001).

3. Myrna Lofthus, *A Spiritual Approach to Astrology* (Sebastopol, CA: CRCS Publications, 1983).

4. Marianne Williamson, *A Return to Love: Reflections on the Principles of A Course in Miracles* (New York: Harper Collins, 1992), ch. 7, section 3, http://www.skdesigns.com/internet/articles/quotes/williamson. html. (Note: This quote is sometimes erroneously attributed to Nelson Mandela.)

CHAPTER THIRTEEN

Tenth House:
It's Lonely at the Top

At the apex of the house wheel is the Tenth House, which in the Equal House system is also the location for the MC, *or Medium Coeli* (literally, the "middle of the sky" in Latin). This is the top of the chart, and if the Sun is here, the person would have been born around midday.

What is the significance of the Tenth House and the MC? Well, here is where we shine like the sun. The Tenth House has to do with public life, status outside the home and in the community, career aspirations, reputation, and ambition. With certain aspects, it could also indicate fame—or infamy. Some astrologers say it is linked with the mother, but I disagree. Perhaps if the mother was the dominant parent in the household this would be the case. I feel the Tenth House has more to do with the father and patriarchal authority figures who affect our lives, for better or worse.

The MC also has to do with "reaching for the top." The house wheel is divided into twelve sections, one for each sign of the zodiac. But, as we learned previously, it is also cut up into quadrants. On the left is the Ascendant (where the sun was rising when the subject was born), and on the right is the Descendant (sunset). These two positions have to do with the horizon—they are the "latitudes" of the house wheel. On the other hand, the MC and the *Imum Coeli* (the IC) are the vertical lines, the meridians, the "longitudes" of the wheel. The MC is at the top, and the IC is at the bottom.

The IC is associated with the Fourth House, which has to do with the home, hearth, domestic life, our parents, and our family heritage. It's the foundation from which we go forth in the world. If the IC is the ground beneath our feet, then the MC is the sky above our heads, the heavens, what we are reaching for. And it's different for every person, thanks in part to what planets live in the Tenth House and what sign is on the cusp. Some people reach for the stars, and some are content to live a life centered around less lofty pursuits.

In her irreverent and wise, all-encompassing tome *Secrets from a Stargazer's Notebook*, author Debbi Kempton-Smith suggests an easy way to remember the symbolism of the MC: just say it out loud, and you have "emcee"—the Master of Ceremonies.[1]

What do we think of when we imagine a master of ceremonies? It's someone who has an extroverted personality, who is always "up" (sometimes irritatingly so), who exists in a theatrical or stagey way. We don't know the "inner" person, but we can usually identify the outer persona—like a movie or rock star. Many people love Katie Couric and her chirpy, girl-next-door TV persona. But do you believe she is like that away from the cameras? No way. You don't get a multimillion-dollar contract and the anchor's seat at a top-rated network by being a sweetie pie. She must have gonads of steel, to put it bluntly. I wonder what sign is on her Tenth House. Martha Stewart has her Sun there, with Leo on the cusp of the Tenth House, and she comes across with warmth and hospitality, as everyone's favorite creative homemaker—who just happens to rule a media empire. That's the Tenth House—it's more about outer appearances than the inner self.

In addition, the sign on the Tenth-House cusp often indicates what kind of career the person might choose—perhaps academia or adventure for Sagittarius, health care for Virgo, some kind of maritime profession for Pisces, and so on.

In studying a person's natal chart and analyzing the complexities of the personality, astrologers will often look at the Sun sign, the Ascendant, the Moon, and then planets in the Tenth House. The Tenth House is that important. Challenging aspects to any planets there are also of great significance, and they will most likely act as roadblocks to the progression of one's career. In midlife, especially, individuals with an active Tenth House will be examining their place in the world, questioning whether they have achieved the goals they had imagined or if they are still struggling beneath karmic influences or challenging aspects.

For example, I have a client named Kim, with the Sun in the Tenth House, opposed by Saturn in the Fourth. She has a frustrating and negative relationship with her father, which suggests some kind of karma. Although she has a brilliant mind, was a good student, and has always been a hard worker, her parents seemed to relate to and encourage another sibling. Kim's sibling became a kind of clone of the parents, adhering to their tastes, parroting their opinions, following in the family business, and never straying too far from the family script. The narcissistic dynamic in the family rewarded the older sib for her "good behavior."

My client, on the other hand, seemed to have just been born to be different. A naturally creative and curious person, Kim gravitated toward artists and other folks who stood in stark contrast to her conservative family. She tried to make her way in the world, in a variety of artistic and public endeavors, but was discouraged by her father and older sister. They humiliated her at the worst, or ignored her at the least. "You'll just get married," they said.

With that Sun in the Tenth House driving her, though, Kim put her nose to the grindstone and tried to ignore her family, receiving little or no encouragement but a lot of sarcastic remarks. She was drawn to the communications industry, and made some inroads there, but found when she looked around the office that her colleagues had come out of the gate much earlier and had a crucial leg up because of the support they had received from their families.

"Why couldn't my father back me up like that?" she wondered. "I would be so much farther along if I'd had some help, at least some pats on the back from him."

It is apparent to me that Kim is working through karma with her father, especially. People with a Tenth-House Sun or Saturn should note that the residue of previous lives will color their public persona and offer many lessons. One of the most powerful of these lessons of the Tenth House is that, sometimes to fulfill our personal potential, we have to break ties with "tribal" or family consciousness. We have to move beyond the family's fears and limitations, and lead our own lives as mature, individuated adults. If we stay too rooted (Fourth House), we block our own growth. Indeed, a Tenth-House Sun can also indicate individuals who remain loyal to a tribe or family that doesn't nurture them, long beyond the usefulness of such ties.

One of Kim's big lessons was that she looked too frequently for her father's approval. Late in life, she realized that he had some of his own foibles and flaws. When we're young, we think our parents are perfect, but of course, they are only human—like everyone else. She understands now that she is a focused, sane person, with a deep reservoir of strength and character.

An activated Tenth House also asks us to "be good"—to use our gifts for the betterment of society rather than self-promotion and power.

Misuse of the Tenth-House gifts will come back to bite us in the behind, either in this life or the next. People with challenging aspects to the Tenth House, or such planets as Mars and Neptune there, should take care to avoid lying or speaking badly of others in order to make themselves look better. Neptune in the Tenth House with squares or oppositions from other planets, for example, could indicate problems due to karma from slandering someone in a previous life. Now, these folks must guard their own reputations in order to balance the karma. Since this placement gives these people charisma, and therefore they may be in the public eye, it is recommended that they be benevolent public figures. Sooner or later, any negative acts will return to haunt them.

People with a Tenth-House Mars must watch their tendency toward a bad temper. As the old saying goes, "Be kind to people on the way up, because these are the same folks you will meet on the way down."

One of the most powerful planets to occupy the Tenth House is Saturn. In fact, the Tenth House, ruled by Capricorn, is the natural place on the wheel for this slow-moving planet. Finding Saturn here might be cause for some reflection, as this is a placement that indicates truly tyrannical—or compassionate—behavior. It all depends on whether the owner chooses to use the power with humility or to wield the dictator's sword.

Adolf Hitler had Saturn here, and we all know how we feel about him. I would love to put Hitler "on the couch," but that would take up way too much space. Some historians theorize that his hatred for Jews originated when, as an art student, Jewish critics dismissed his youthful artwork as being trite and sentimental. Others wonder what kind of parents he had.

Saturn in the Tenth House often points to an absent parent, one who might have died young or abandoned the family, leaving the children to be raised by an older surrogate, such as a grandparent. Individuals with this placement will need to take responsibility early

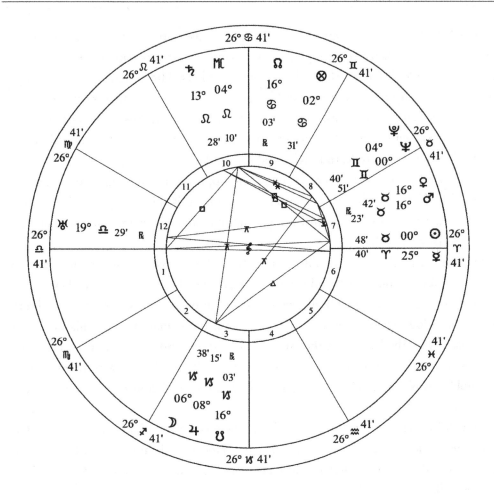

Adolf Hitler
April 20, 1889 / 6:30 p.m. Local Mean Time
Time Zone: 0 hours West
Braunau am Inn, Austria / Equal Houses

on. One of the more positive outcomes of a Tenth-House Saturn is that these people will mature sooner than their peers. Neglectful or absent parents motivate them to take their lives seriously, to look out for themselves as well as others. They might "parent" younger siblings and grow up to be very responsible and protective parents themselves. They will also look out for employees, constituents, and, if in the military, those of lesser rank.

Those with a Tenth-House Saturn can assume immense responsibilities, sometimes too many, in fact. They need to learn to relax and spread the work around.

Although youth may have been a struggle and opportunities seemed hard to come by, the powerful will of a Tenth-House Saturn can overcome this. These people will make their own opportunities, persevering until things truly blossom for them. Their middle years will be especially fruitful.

Once they've reached the top, folks with a Tenth-House Saturn must remember to be fair. Sometimes this placement indicates too great a need for authority, so these people need to avoid being too dictatorial, whether at home or in the workplace. Also, Tenth-House Saturn does not let them rest on their laurels. Individuals with this placement can pat themselves on the back once they've achieved success and step away from the grindstone, but they don't get to take the rest of their lives off. That's okay with them, though. These noble people thrive on meaningful work, and they will continue to pursue it until they are quite old.

Many individuals with this placement have taken Saturn's wisdom and courage and led creative, inspirational lives. Yes, Hitler and J. Edgar Hoover had Saturn in the Tenth House, but so did Abraham Lincoln and Timothy Leary. Bill Clinton's Saturn is close to the Tenth House as well.

This points to one of the lessons I stress when I counsel clients: Astrology isn't destiny; it's a blueprint or map for the psyche. We ultimately make the choices as to which roads we take.

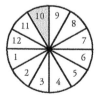

Tenth House: The natural house for Capricorn and ruled by Saturn, the Tenth House has to do with ambition and aspirations, public image, honor, rank, authority figures, and responsibility. This is where the *Medium Coeli* is located.

Planets in the Tenth House

Sun in the Tenth House

Born around midday, these folks have the ability to shine like the sun. If well aspected, this is the placement of the executive and the leader, the one who has the courage to rise to the top. Success is very important to people with a Tenth-House Sun, and it is not always personal power that motivates them—they truly desire to inspire others to find their own way up the mountain. The Tenth House has to do with Saturn and is the natural house for Capricorn, so picture a mountain goat picking its way up the rocky climes. There is a likelihood of karmic issues with the father or a father figure.

Moon in the Tenth House

With the right intentions and enough focus, these people could make excellent public servants—the kind of people who can make a difference, helping the electorate or those working for them. They're ambitious and have personality-plus and a desire to help and serve society.

Mercury in the Tenth House

This is another position that favors travel and brings the native a talent for communications, oral and written. In fact, these people may travel as part of their professional lives. Their minds are busy and alert, but because of Capricorn's influence (the natural sign on the cusp of the Tenth House), these individuals will have a more practical and steady nature than those with Mercury placed elsewhere. This would be the placement for a political speechwriter or the chief of staff for a government official.

Venus in the Tenth House

This is a good position for someone who needs to inspire the public with words—an excellent orator, singer, or other kind of entertainer who uses his or her voice. This placement implies a positive financial life and an overall sense of optimism.

Mars in the Tenth House

We analyze the Tenth House when we look for powerful karma, and indeed, with Mars here there might be the need to balance the tendency in a previous life to be manipulative, to speak ill of others for personal gain—like smearing the opponent in a political campaign. There may also be challenging issues with the father. Otherwise, this is the placement for a successful entrepreneur, because people with this position have great ambition combined with energy.

Jupiter in the Tenth House

Appealing, almost irresistible in nature, these folks are fortunate because positions of power seem to fall in their laps, but deservedly so, unless there are other factors in the chart. Honorable people with a Tenth-House Jupiter bring their karmic gifts into this incarnation to benefit society. A desire for achievement, plus a strong work ethic paired with Jupiter's optimism, makes for people who are naturally attractive to business and professional partners.

Saturn in the Tenth House

This placement is the mark of ambitious, hard-working, responsible individuals who are not afraid to persevere through periods of disappointment to reach their goals. Their natural conservatism could be balanced by a more breezy, lighthearted Sun, Moon, or rising sign. There may have been childhood challenges with the father or dominant parent. For a man, perhaps the father was away working a lot and the young Tenth-House Saturn had to be the "little man" around the house. Some astrologers tsk-tsk when they see Saturn in the Tenth, whispering, "You know, Hitler had Saturn there." And indeed, there is karma here, related to the misuse of authority in a previous life. I prefer to remind folks with this placement—who have a tremendous ability to rise from humble beginnings to positions of great power—to use their Saturnian wisdom when they achieve positions of authority, and lead with kindness and fairness. The great, wise Ram Dass also has this placement. Saturn in Tenth is an excellent position for a career in business, as well as medicine, science, and research.

Uranus in the Tenth House

How about a career in metaphysics? This placement suggests some kind of unusual line of business as well as decisions about the career that may have to be made very suddenly. This is not the position for drudgery. Folks with a Tenth-House Uranus need to be original and inventive in the workplace and with life in general. Their innovations could lead them to the pinnacle of success.

Neptune in the Tenth House

These idealistic folks are naturally suited to professions where they can help people, whether as a psychologist, assisting others through rough spots in their psyches, or as a makeup artist or hairdresser, helping others feel more beautiful. Medicine or other humanitarian positions would also suit those with Neptune in the Tenth House. People with this placement might not always get the public recognition they deserve, but whatever good works they humbly do will go into the "karmic vault" and build valuable credit for future incarnations. They have unusually accessible connections to the etheric and angelic realms, and although they may not know it, they have spirit guides very close to them.

Pluto in the Tenth House

This is a powerful and perplexing placement for Pluto. Here are the saints working for the betterment of society, or the individuals who desire power only to satisfy a personal goal, one that might not be in society's best interests. Or perhaps these folks will remove themselves from the mainstream, focusing their energies on an intense inner life. The path they choose to take will either resolve or add to their karmic issues.

---

1. Debbi Kempton-Smith, *Secrets from a Stargazer's Notebook* (New York: Topquark Press, 1999), p. 10.

CHAPTER FOURTEEN

Eleventh House:
You've Got to Have Friends

From cults to committees, the Eleventh House has to do with groups and associations. Now we are rounding the stretch of the house wheel, coming south from the "North Pole" of the Tenth House—the pinnacle of self-motivation. If the lower quadrant symbolizes the soul's early development and attitudes learned from the family of origin, and the second quadrant puts them into action creatively and in the workplace, then the third quadrant merges ways of thinking and tests us to see how we can blend all of this with a partner, as well as how we might forge a deeper philosophy about our own lives.

The Tenth House calls us to responsibility in the outside world—career, family, and society at large. It also tests us (sometimes with rewards, sometimes with troubles) to see how we've done with everything we've been given so far. Now it's time to take those values on the road.

Ruled by Uranus and associated with Aquarius, the Eleventh House resonates with those Aquarian principles sung about in the song "The Age of Aquarius," applied to our fellow humanity—harmony, understanding, sympathy, truth. The song is an idealistic, visionary philosophy for a Utopian culture.

Some of us still remember wanting to live that dream, which may have been naïve in the face of the military-industrial complex. We can still see some examples of Aquarian ideals when people join together to rally for social causes such as the environment, civil rights, women's rights, the nuclear disarmament movement, ethical treatment of animals, and awareness of poverty issues.

I saw a spark of that spirit in the peace marches that preceded the Iraq War, and during the 2004 presidential election year—the spirited folks with their clipboards popping up around cities and small towns, urging people to register and vote. Will these efforts do anything to change the country? Only time will tell—but for the individuals involved, all of these Eleventh-House type of things energize them.

Group activities and social activism take us out of ourselves and show how we engage with the community, not just with our close friends or partners but also the world at large.

Interestingly, planets placed in this position or the sign on the cusp can also indicate whether these pursuits are really heartfelt—whether the Eleventh-House person honestly cares about her concerns or she's using the public platform for her own self-promotion. I was a bit too young to have participated in the marches and rallies protesting the Vietnam War, but my husband remembers them well (and has a different slant on things, being a veteran of that war). There were surely many idealistic people who hated the sight of bodies coming home in coffins and the song and dance routine the administration gave us. But my husband, Mr. Cynical, always says a lot of the more opportunistic guys at those events "got more women" than the average Joe who didn't participate (or a short-haired soldier coming home).

Seducing women by using leadership—the kind an organizer of a peace rally might possess—would be a downside of the Eleventh House. The humanitarian interests would take a sideline to the ego's gratification.

I wonder how many charismatic leaders of large social or tribal groups have strong planets in the Eleventh House.

A few of the more benign public figures with planets in the Eleventh House include Timothy Leary, Bill Clinton, Martin Luther King Jr., and Jerry Garcia, the late founder and long-time leader of the Grateful Dead.

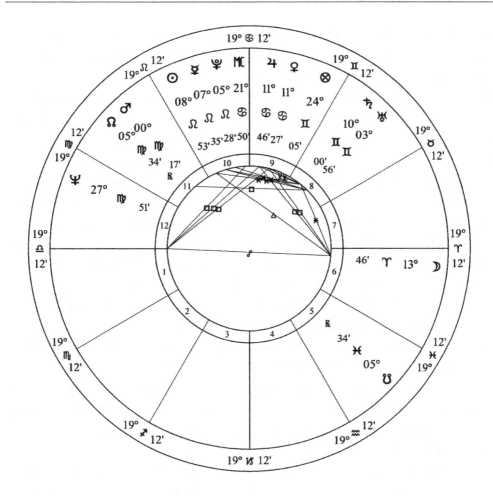

Jerry Garcia
August 1, 1942 / 12:05 p.m. War Time
Time Zone: 8 hours West
San Francisco, CA / Equal Houses

With Mars in the Eleventh House in Virgo, Jerry Garcia had a revolutionary approach to rock music, where the audience and fans merged with the band. He was also a talented, if understated, player and a meticulous organizer.

Perhaps you've seen the bumper stickers that say "Who Are the Grateful Dead and Why Are They Following Me?" My cousin was one such person who might have come to wonder why the Grateful Dead were "following her." I once asked her how many times she'd seen them. "Oh, about 100, 150, maybe 200 times," she said nonchalantly.

Ack! And I thought I was a fanatic because I'd seen Peter Gabriel about eight times.

These fans were not just ordinary concertgoers. A Dead concert was like a tribal ritual, and the followers were a family, with its own special kind of "family values." This is not Mom and Dad and 2.5 children at home behind the picket fence. Serious, diehard Dead-heads carried on some of the best traits left over from the height of the hippie movement—the rejection of materialism, the bohemian "live for the moment" lifestyle, and communal values. There were often improvised kitchens, people bartering food for tickets or money to travel on, handmade crafts, and even al fresco "medicine men"—herbalists helping those who might have had a little too much sunshine and bliss. These selfless kinds of things resonate with the Eleventh House. The dark side, of course, was the substance abuse.

Jerry Garcia, who also had numerous planets in the Tenth House, was the Godfather of all this, whether he wanted to be or not, and even worked himself into ill health running the band and touring. With Mars in the Eleventh House, he was both independent and accessible. People felt like they knew him, like he spoke to them. He was a born leader, someone who could fire up the imagination of legions of fans. There was also a little bit of a mystery about Jerry, and there still is, especially about the last few years before his death. Images of a godlike Garcia and the aesthetic of the Dead live on, as well as bootleg tapes of their concerts. The remaining band members continue to tour and attract what are probably the grandchildren of the original Deadheads, tie-dyed baby clothes and all.

The best part about the Grateful Dead, thanks in part to Garcia but also his long-time drummer, Mickey Hart, is the embracing and championing of world music. As George Harrison introduced Ravi Shankar and Indian classical string music to Beatles fans, Garcia and Hart did the same with percussion. First with the Diga Rhythm Band—the first international percussion-based band of its kind, which included the masterful Zakir Hussain.

Then Planet Drum and countless other side projects helped bring ethnic music from all corners of the world to Western ears.

Music is, indeed, a universal language that brings us together—something that fits in well with the essence of the Eleventh House. Perhaps this might seem more of a Ninth-House phenomenon, but the seeds were planted within the Grateful Dead, and it all started with Jerry Garcia and a little jam band from San Francisco.

The negative side of the Eleventh House comes when these folks put the "world at large" before everyone else, including significant others. People with their Sun there, or a challenging aspect to a planet in the Eleventh House, could identify with the group perhaps too strongly. They could work themselves into a fatigued state (like Jerry Garcia did). They might feel more at home in a group, and sometimes their dedication to their causes might cause them to keep their family or loved ones at arm's length for the sake of their public endeavors. Their coterie and public image could also swallow up their individuality, and they could sublimate their identity for the sake of the group, not daring to let the tribe down by asking for their own needs to be fulfilled.

Still, I believe that people with a strong Eleventh House—several planets there, or the Sun, Moon, or rising sign in Aquarius—keep the better juices of humanity going. They're the opposite of the greedheads, who act without scruples, ruin the environment, and lay off people from their jobs in order to make more and more—and more—money. In Buddhism, feeding this insatiable need for material acquisition is called chasing "the hungry ghost." Unfortunately, it's sort of the essence of capitalism.

We need Eleventh-House folks and Aquarians to counterbalance this lust for individual profit.

Planets in the Eleventh House and/or planets in Aquarius give these folks a heartfelt need to do good for their fellow humans, whether it's Benjamin Franklin (Moon and Mercury in the Eleventh) donating the technology of the lightning rod to society to help prevent fires, or a contemporary person taking time away from work and family to help run a local charity.

I have a manager, an Aquarius, who sits on so many committees at work and within the community that I don't know when she finds the time to sleep.

And she does look tired sometimes. She really is a kind person, though, and doesn't do this for "the resume," but because helping others resonates for her. One of her charitable groups raises money to bring music lessons and musical instruments to children in lower-income families.

Around the office, sometimes we get cynical, especially if there are cutbacks, wage freezes, and old clunky technology. My manager stays positive and finds small ways to keep the team, the group (Eleventh House), afloat, even in the face of hardship.

If it was me during times of downsizing, I would just leave early, call in sick more, and stay home and play with my cats. But that's why I'm not a manager!

My point is, people with an activated Eleventh House may become too engrossed in office and charity work, to the detriment of their intimate relationships, their physical health, and even their own soul's growth. We first have to fix what's inside of us and love what is right next to us before we can save the world.

 ***Eleventh House:*** The natural house for Aquarius and ruled by Uranus, the Eleventh House has to do with shared pleasures, hobbies and group interests, communal causes and movements, and futuristic visions.

Planets in the Eleventh House

Sun in the Eleventh House

This is the natural house for Aquarius, which means a strong planet like the Sun here would give the person a humanitarian and progressive outlook on life, with a desire to rise above the mundane or petty aspects of life, seeking higher awareness and higher consciousness. These folks have a lot of energy to give to groups and are naturally popular.

Moon in the Eleventh House

Popular and sensitive, these are good folks to lean on and good friends to the quiet people who might be unpopular themselves—who really need someone to hear and support them. Like union shop stewards or block leaders, they will take responsibility for and support a group effort rather than promote themselves.

Mercury in the Eleventh House

These folks need friends who have keen minds, talent, and an interest in "what's out there." These are not your average guys and gals smoking cigarettes around the kitchen table and gossiping about the folks who live downstairs. They're more interested in what's happening globally and would like to use their considerable intellect to help the world or improve things in the bigger picture. They may go far if they can channel their sometimes-scattered mental abilities.

Venus in the Eleventh House

Folks with this placement are fortunate and popular. They are the men or women with a gaggle of loyal friends, which is well deserved because they have a natural inclination toward graciousness, generosity, and tact. You always feel at ease around those with an Eleventh-House Venus. The flip side is, they may give too much energy taking care of or comforting others. They need to learn to draw boundaries.

Mars in the Eleventh House

These people expend a lot of energy around friends and in groups, which may include a variety of people. There can be a bit too much "flexibility" when it comes to choosing pals. This placement reminds me of a quadruple-Aquarius client who would occasionally bring a homeless person to dinner, much to his wife's chagrin. More likely, individuals with Mars in the Eleventh might be too trusting, bringing a con man (or woman) home to dinner. If you have this placement, use wisdom in choosing your friends.

Jupiter in the Eleventh House

Generous and broad-minded, these people are among the luckiest when it comes to sheer enjoyment of life. Some of us may remember that there was always a popular crowd in high school (and some of us may have not been included in that group), and I'll bet many of these folks had some kind of beneficent planet, such as Jupiter, in the "friendship house." The flip side is that being distracted by busyness and social stroking takes a person away from self-examination and doing one's inner work.

Saturn in the Eleventh House

Friends will come and go in these people's lives, and their group efforts will need to be just that—for the group. They can't rely on personal recognition but should take satisfaction in "doing it for the greater good." Here is another placement that suggests a "heavy" life as a youth, which will lighten up as these people grow older—that is, if they do the work, tap their considerable inner strength, and, especially, have faith.

Uranus in the Eleventh House

These people will work for the betterment of the group, usually toward an unusual, revolutionary goal. Friends come and go, sometimes very suddenly. Perhaps because of the disappointment connected with the sudden loss of a close friend, these people prefer to have a network of colleagues instead of one or two best friends.

Neptune in the Eleventh House

These folks need to watch out for false friends. The trusting, fluid nature of Neptune in the house of friendship and groups could allow these people to fall in with the wrong people or open their hearts (and homes and wallets) to "friends" who will hurt or deceive them. They need to be discerning in choosing their comrades. Happily, with discretion, they could find themselves with pals who are gifted in a variety of ways. They also need to focus on pinning down their goals. They have great humanitarian dreams, but often lack the motivation or energy to achieve them. Those with an Eleventh-House Neptune might like to adopt a philosophy such as "a journey begins with the first step."

Pluto in the Eleventh House

Pluto in the house of group energy gives these natives a natural ability to influence a wide range of people, and it's up to them whether they choose to use this ability for higher or base purposes. Pluto has to do with transformation, so people with this placement will have a desire to change society through friends, groups, and associations. Think of the folks who protested environmental negligence (and mainstream culture) by going back to the Earth. Such communal living, especially if it makes a statement, appeals to those with an Eleventh-House Pluto. Intense, insightful, and loyal, these folks may belong to many groups but have only a few intimate friends. However, these friendships will last a lifetime.

CHAPTER FIFTEEN

Twelfth House:
The Sound of One Hand Clapping

Traditionally, the Twelfth House, ruled by Neptune, is linked with prisons, slavery, bond-age, large institutions, hospitals, hidden enemies, self-destruction, escapist tendencies, exile, addictions, self-delusion, and even procrastination. I think the old stereotypes are unfortu-nate. Essentially, the astrological traditions say that there is a variety of mental, physical, creative, and ego restrictions for a person with an activated Twelfth House.

I'd like to bring these issues more into the twenty-first century—the age of contempo-rary psychology and postmodern metaphor. This changes and somewhat disarms the doom and gloom of this house, especially for people who have their Sun or several planets there.

Yes, it can be a harbinger of challenges, but there also are positive elements to the Twelfth House. When we study past lives, we begin to understand how a loaded Twelfth House has to do with karma and reincarnation. A person with a stellium of planets here is going to a kind of graduate school—maybe even getting a Ph.D.—in spiritual growth. This is probably an old soul who is getting ready to make a big leap in consciousness—not that this is the person's last time around on the Earth plane, but he or she is getting close. Perhaps a series of "easy incarnations" has made the soul lazy about learning and doing the inner work. Many planets in the Twelfth House, especially if they're not well aspected—inconjuncts, oppositions, squares, etc.—indicate that there are many lessons to learn.

It would be best not to sleep through this class, this incarnation. But if we pay attention and master the challenges, the rewards will be brilliant.

Along with difficulties, a busy Twelfth House also brings gifts from above. There are blessings here, such as guardian angels, rich, symbolic dreams, intuitions, synchronicity, and all that is related to mysticism and the unconscious. Frequently, there is psychic strength, including the ability to heal. The past, especially the distant, karmic past, is "in the house" here too. "How can I serve God?" and "What is my soul's purpose?" are two questions that probably best summarize the selfless service of the Twelfth House.

Keep these positive things in mind if you look at your chart and see powerful planets in the Twelfth. This house is misunderstood and frequently quite scary because of all those references to prisons, hospitals, and institutions.

People born with many planets in the Twelfth House may read some of the older astrology texts and think they're doomed to the county lockup or the psychiatric ward. No way. These folks shouldn't give up and be prepared for a long hospital stay or get used to an orange jumpsuit. Instead, they should be wise and toe the line with the law—and take care and control of their psychological health. A crowded Twelfth House, with its emphasis on psychology, would suggest that these natives use wisdom in handling their emotions. They could learn about cognitive behavioral therapy, for example—using the intellect to think through and gain mastery over destructive feelings.

Or, with a planet or more here, such individuals might find themselves employed in a prison or hospital. Physicians frequently have planets in the Twelfth House.

My sister has her Mars in the Twelfth, in the sign of Taurus. After leaving a lay teaching position in a parochial school, she has found success working with and teaching people who are incarcerated. They like her very much, and she has won awards for her abilities. Interestingly, she brings relaxing, beautiful music to her students (that's the Taurus/Venus connection). She says they have been open to this and that it seems to have a calming effect.

Someone has to take care of people who are incarcerated, who probably landed in jail because of a childhood filled with neglect. Perhaps with caring, they will have a second chance. That's one of the best manifestations of a Twelfth-House planet placement. My sister will never be rich or famous for her efforts, but it's good, heart-centered work.

In a sadder but enlightening Twelfth-House story, a client and friend of mine was troubled to find her Venus there, in challenging aspect to the Moon. Indeed, there was a lot of heartache in her life, especially concerning women. A distant mother seemed to set the stage for low self-esteem, lack of self-love, and shyness. (An afflicted Venus in the Twelfth House often makes the native shy.) So, friends were hard to come by too.

In one of the most unfortunate manifestations of a Twelfth-House Venus, my client was subject to sexual misconduct from an adult family friend—not out-and-out abuse, but certainly behavior that was untoward. When told, her mother rolled her eyes and sighed in disbelief.

The real downside of this was my friend's inability to feel supported or protected by her mother. She also felt overly sexualized at a young age, and thus had conflicting ideas about sex and love.

My client also had a vivid imagination and found herself falling in love with people who were unavailable, even make-believe lovers like movie and rock stars. She used her imagination to conjure elaborate story lines around these charismatic figures. This is also a mark of Venus in the Twelfth House—the fiction writer.

As she matured, she realized that these flights of fancy and bad habits were not helping her grow in any way. She eventually settled down with a low-key man who reached her heart and her creative soul.

My client has come to accept the challenges associated with a Twelfth-House Venus that happen with romantic, human love and has focused on giving and receiving love in a broader, universal sense, studying spiritual healing and body work. She actively studies dreams and intuition and works with the angelic realms, which enhance her creativity.

Instead of the self-aggrandizing behavior of her youth—destructive love affairs, parties, overspending—she's turned the "locked-up" love energy of the Twelfth-House Venus inward, seeking to understand her soul's purpose and how to communicate and disseminate spiritual ideas to help others in need.

That's the way challenging aspects or difficult placements in the Twelfth House work. They instruct and give choices, but never doom us to imprisonment of the psyche.

The astrological chart is like a blueprint for the soul's present incarnation. We can follow the "design" and just stay with it, have a structure that is built at birth and never changes, or we can find the weaknesses in that structure and make improvements or renovations, just like in a building. Sometimes we can even take down the structure to its foundation and rebuild it.

Edgar Cayce said, "The spirit is the life, the mind is the builder and physical is the result."[1] He added that the birth chart exists as a plan—but never as one's destiny. The will, combined with an ideal of the soul's purpose, can rise above any circumstances, even a grouping of troublesome planets in the Twelfth House.

So, you might rethink the traditional astrological interpretation that having planets in the Twelfth House means a brush with incarceration. (The best way to avoid jail is, of course, to stay on the right side of the law.) I prefer to think of imprisonment more as a metaphor. We can imprison ourselves with our thoughts, or we can free ourselves.

In her online column for *InnerSelf*, astrologer and writer Dana Gerhardt writes: "In structuring your Twelfth House psyche, you have infinite choices. You can, like the young Dalai Lama in Potala, roam an inner residence a quarter-mile long with a thousand rooms, enjoying this precious incarnation, and taking advantage of centuries of learning from vast inner libraries. Or you can pace a small prison cell of past mistakes. Or you can lie upon a sick bed of wounds. Whether your Twelfth feels like a temple, a prison or a hospital is your choice."[2]

Now let's look at a couple of famous folks, both with a Twelfth-House Sun.

There's Dubya—President Number 43—George W. Bush.

Love him or hate him, his rise to the presidency is surrounded by mystery and intrigue—Twelfth-House stuff. Secrecy and family connections, especially with the father, surround his administration. Think of the 2000 election itself. ("The election isn't over until your brother counts the votes," as one bumper sticker said.) Did the Bush family have anything to do with disenfranchising a number of lower income Democratic voters in north Florida? How come all those elderly Jewish ladies in Palm Beach County voted for Pat Buchanan when they obviously wanted to vote for "their Joey," Joe Lieberman, Al Gore's running mate?

And what of Bush himself? The Sun in this position suggests wavering with oneself early on, not being able to get off the mark or find a purpose in life. George W. Bush has been questioned about his stint in the armed forces. At Yale, he was admittedly a lackluster student and battled alcohol and drugs later on. Yet things seemed to turn around when he became a born-again Christian, which probably gave him a rudder to steer his life. The Twelfth House can connect us to mystical experiences, such as a religious epiphany.

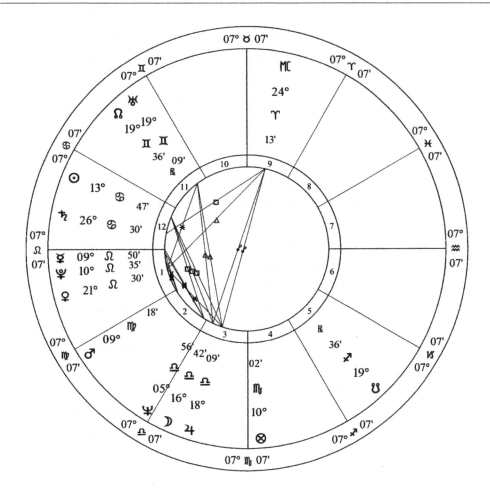

George W. Bush
July 6, 1946 / 9:51 a.m. Daylight Saving Time
Time Zone: 5 hours West
New Haven, CT / Equal Houses

However, this is also cloaked in uncertainty. Bush speaks frequently about his personal connection with Christ, but his talk is so dogmatic. It's as if he's saying, "Christ, GOOD, everyone else, BAD." ("You're with us or against us.") Does he really feel the presence of Christ in his heart, or is he just trying to bolster himself in the polls by appeasing his Christian fundamentalist supporters? There's that Neptunian/Twelfth-House camouflage, like octopus ink. Mysteries just keep piling up with this president. Only history will reveal the truth.

History, however, has told the tale of Abraham Lincoln, who had his Moon in the Twelfth House, and the Sun right on the cusp between the Twelfth and First Houses.

Lincoln was known for his melancholia, his difficult marriage, and the tragic loss of two sons. Writings suggest that Lincoln had to sneak into Washington for his inauguration. The presidential train ran through Baltimore, which was in the border state of Maryland, and there was an assassination attempt on the president-elect. Lincoln feared for his life, simply to get into office.[3] That's the Twelfth-House theme of secret enemies.

More profoundly—and very reflective of the Twelfth House—Lincoln executed one of the most symbolic deeds in our nation's history: freeing the slaves. The Emancipation Proclamation allowed African-American men, women, and children to shrug off their literal bondage (Twelfth House) and find the road to freedom.

In addition, although Lincoln is admired now, he was obviously hated at the time—assassinated at Ford's Theater by John Wilkes Booth . . . a secret enemy. It is said that he foresaw his own death, dreaming of a body in a coffin, only to realize it was his own. All of these elements in Lincoln's life—the link to slavery, the foes, and his psychic awareness—resonate with traditional aspects of the Twelfth House.

Finally, Lincoln bore the mark of the Twelfth House with the solitude he endured educating himself. He also possessed considerable writing abilities—take the Gettysburg Address, for example.

Lincoln was able to soothe the nation's grief through his words, in a brief, elegant piece of writing. I believe his Twelfth-House planets helped Lincoln feel the ineffable quality of Gettysburg. His great soul understood the numinous sorrow of the blood-soaked fields and the soldiers who fought there.

In a minimal amount of words, Lincoln channeled all of those profound feelings and emotions through his pen. Almost magically, he put it all together with the Gettysburg Address, which would forever honor the souls of the dead and inspire future generations to remember them, as well as the lessons of war.

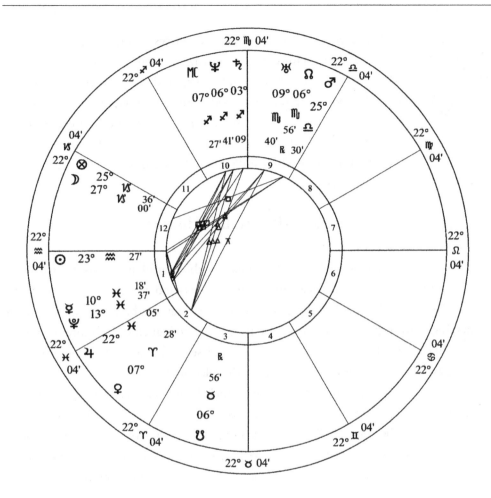

Abraham Lincoln
February 12, 1809 / 6:54 a.m. Local Mean Time
Time Zone: 0 hours West
Hodgenville, KY / Equal Houses

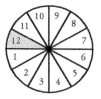

Twelfth House: The natural house for Pisces and governed by Neptune, the Twelfth House has to do with hospitals, prisons, monasteries, and other large institutions; bondage and confinement, included being "locked up" in one's own bad habits and thought patterns; psychology and psychiatry; positive and negative methods of escapism; the past, including the very distant past of karma; and psychic gifts, such as hands-on healing skills, the unconscious, the mystical, and the metaphysical.

Planets in the Twelfth House

Sun in the Twelfth House

This is a position of extremes—whether these folks are thoughtful and introspective or totally self-serving depends on the placement of other planets and aspects in the chart. With the Sun in the Twelfth House, healthy growth of the ego may not be encouraged early on in life, making it difficult to "get out of the starting gate," to launch oneself into the public sphere in adulthood. The native may be retiring and self-effacing or a real in-your-face type. Everyday saints and egomaniacs both have this placement.

For example, both Gandhi and Madonna have their Suns here. Need we say more? One individual was willing to starve himself to death to free his country, and the other—well, she makes no bones about being "The Material Girl." It's sacrifice versus self-promotion.

Eventually, these people must find their path by themselves, learning the hard way to get along with others, preferring to retreat to private pursuits and give their heart to a small coterie of friends.

If the ego is exaggerated, there is a "with us or against us" attitude. Again, think of George W. Bush and his speech before launching the Iraq invasion—countries that questioned the rationale for going to war (such as France) were suddenly not our "friends" anymore.

The more enlightened types will often work tirelessly for the underdog, or in large institutions such as prisons, schools, or hospitals.

Moon in the Twelfth House

Like those with the Moon in Pisces, these individuals possess great sensitivity and kindness. However, when pushed too far or asked for too much support, they will withdraw or just give superficial support. They truly feel your pain, and sometimes it's just too much for them to bear.

People with the Moon in the Twelfth have strong feelings, but also have the need to hide them away. This may be because early in life they needed to prop up a weak or depressed parent, especially the mother.

My father has this placement. During the Depression, my grandfather had to find work in another state and came home to be with the family only a few times a year. My father, the youngest child, was the only one left at home and watched my grandmother, understandably, become very depressed. I think he was trying to be strong for her and absorbed the idea of "not making waves" with his emotions.

As a result, he developed a kind of cheerful mask, one that is charming but can be frustrating if you're trying to probe some deeper issues. He kept smiling through my mother's long illness, when sometimes I wanted to scream or sob. We had to keep our feelings—especially pain and sorrow—in check.

This can be a lonely position, too. Women especially may shy away from the pleasures of love, fearing the turmoil that can come with intense emotions.

The Moon in the Twelfth House gives a special sense of insight into spiritual and metaphysical matters, though, and is a useful placement for writers, psychologists, and detectives.

There also is a love for learning and a special affinity for children. These people may in fact be childlike, with a sweet, appealing nature and a youthful appearance.

Mercury in the Twelfth House

With this placement there are problems with self-acceptance, and the seeds may have been sown in childhood, through a lack of love. People with a Twelfth-House Mercury may have grown up in tough circumstances, perhaps where the family was so stressed and focused on survival issues that there was no time for nurturing. Or the parents could have lacked the emotional tools to show love and impart a healthy sense of self.

These folks may grow into the type that lives in a world of fantasy, through things like romantic movies, gossip magazines, and soap operas. If badly aspected, this position could make the person a gossip, a know-it-all, or just generally nosy. These people could also be inclined toward overdoing it with food, alcohol, and drugs—anything to cloud reality. Self-awareness is very hard to cultivate, but if it is, the more enlightened types will seek counseling, read self-help books, or consult an astrologer in an attempt to understand themselves.

Venus in the Twelfth House

Cue Doris Day: "Once I had a secret love . . ."

This is the placement for secret, intriguing love affairs or for living in a romantic world of fantasy, even admiring someone—who may be unavailable—from afar. Often the lover will be much older, a person who gives the sense of parental nurturing these folks lacked in youth.

People with a Twelfth-House Venus may have to overcome severe shyness, which could lead them to fall in love with the first person who pays attention to them.

Depending on which planets are here, as well as the aspects, they could harm themselves by overdoing with drugs, food, alcohol, or spending, as well as pursuing unhealthy love affairs. Taken to the extreme, these pastimes could lead to a brush with the law or could bring on ill health.

At the very worst, this placement could suggest the baser aspects of love and sex—promiscuity, sexual abuse, bondage, and fetishes. These natives may have suffered sexual abuse as a child or may have been neglected in matters of the heart.

Learning to love yourself is the best way to work through this challenging placement of Venus. Serving or loving in a broad, universal way—championing the underdog, working with those who can't help themselves, even working with animals—is one way to take the high road with Venus in the Twelfth House. The gurus always say that if you are lonely, finding meaningful work or service—something that makes you "shine" inside—is the best way to attract others.

In addition, on the positive side, this is also a good placement for fiction writing, particularly romances. Venus in the Twelfth House can also indicate the presence of guardian angels.

Mars in the Twelfth House

Like the backstage crew at a theater or the trusted public relations agent for a superstar, these folks are usually in the background in some way, letting those who are more extroverted get "out there." Sometimes this is by choice—these folks like to put their energies into being great support systems for others. But this placement can also indicate individuals whose sense of self was shut down early on in life, discouraged from allowing themselves to individuate.

These people may have a hard time standing up for themselves in times of difficulty, because of the lack of support in their childhood environment. This could lead to passive-aggressive behavior.

Or, these folks could hold in their anger until it builds to a critical mass, then explode and express themselves in destructive ways. This unhealthy venting is where those with a Twelfth-House Mars get in trouble—sometimes even with the law. Better to let out steam little by little than let it build up until you're mad enough to punch someone.

With challenging aspects, these individuals might also try to numb their tamped-down anger with drugs, alcohol, food, or other substances. If you find this placement of Mars in your chart and you have a tendency toward negative behavior and habits, learn to understand the emotions, through cognitive behavioral therapy, anger management books or classes, or the help of a support group.

People with Mars in the Twelfth House can also harness their abundant energy to fight for the underdog or a special cause. They can put their strength into healthy physical activities. Martial arts, yoga, and tai chi are especially positive, because they connect the body and "belly" energy with mental discipline and spiritual awareness—channeling the tremendous energy from the lower chakras right up through the crown.

Jupiter in the Twelfth House

Associated with good fortune when placed in the other houses, Jupiter does provide luck if found in the Twelfth House—but it has limitations. Jupiter's beneficence will assist these folks in times of trouble, helping them weather crises that might crush another person.

However, the bounty of Jupiter is hampered in the Twelfth House. These are the kind-hearted people who "throw their pearls before swine," giving way too much to others and

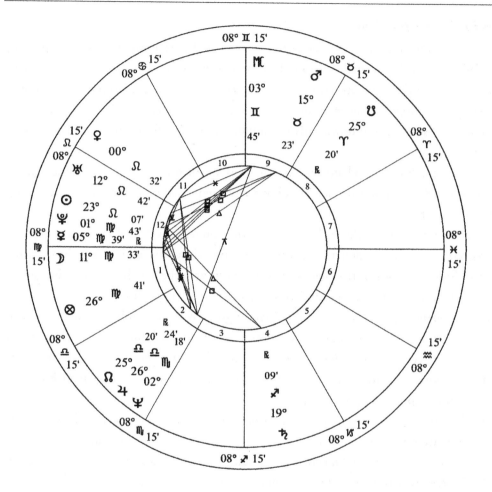

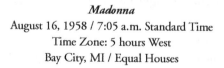

Madonna
August 16, 1958 / 7:05 a.m. Standard Time
Time Zone: 5 hours West
Bay City, MI / Equal Houses

running the risk of being used. The realization of this hurts them so much that they may become bitter and withdrawn.

Perhaps there is a karmic lesson here—these folks may have taken advantage of others in a previous life. Now they are balancing this karma.

Saturn in the Twelfth House

This is the placement of little men and little women. Childhood circumstances may have forced these individuals to grow up quickly. They adopt an adult attitude early in life and an outer persona of seriousness and conventionality.

With its links to hospitals, Saturn placed here is the mark of the dedicated doctor or surgeon. Saturn gives the drive and discipline to make it through medical school, for one thing, but also imparts a sincere desire to help others. In addition, people with a Twelfth-House Saturn possess the work ethic necessary to thrive in this chaotic and demanding profession.

There is also a detachment that allows these people to create emotional distance and protect themselves from the turmoil and suffering encountered in a hospital.

The Twelfth is the house of karma, and Saturn has been called the "Lord of Karma," so this planet is quite at home here.

Uranus in the Twelfth House

Folks with this placement were usually discouraged early on from expressing their individuality. But if the family tries to rein in this wildcat, they just might get clawed. People with a Twelfth-House Uranus can't help themselves—they'll be outstanding and unusual in some way.

This could be the kid in class or the person at the office who always wears a hat, for example, or red cowboy boots—or a lapel button with a radical slogan.

We mentioned Madonna before.

Along with her Sun and Mars, Madonna has Uranus here, in Leo. Everyone probably knows about her difficult childhood in a large, strict Catholic family, losing her mother at a young age. The challenges were great, but Madonna was driven to make her mark, even if as a girl it was transforming her Catholic school uniform into a trendy miniskirt.

It took a lot of guts to get to New York City and then to international fame, but Madonna was up to the task. Although she can be very self-serving, she is obviously about as much of an individual as you'll encounter. One of her biggest hits was the song "Express Your-self"—that's Uranus in the Twelfth.

Critics may argue her worth, but Madonna brought about a lot of change in women's roles in popular music. Suddenly women in pop and rock could be "the boss," not just backup vocalists or demure singer-songwriters.

Madonna's timing was excellent, too. She blew into the public eye thanks mostly to her exposure on MTV, especially her unforgettable performance of "Like a Virgin" at the 1985 Video Music Awards ceremony. (Remember her costume—a wedding dress?)

Uranus rules electronic media, and Madonna connected with a worldwide audience more through her creative videos than her music. She's also fascinating because of her canny knowledge of marketing as well as her ability to keep reinventing herself. Uranus has to do with trends and inventions, and interestingly, Madonna's 2004 world tour was called "The Re-invention Tour."

There's an unforgettable, one-of-a-kind quality to her. She named her record company Maverick. That's Madonna (and Twelfth-House Uranus) in a nutshell.

On the other hand, if poorly aspected, Twelfth-House Uranus could be the mark of the charismatic, brilliant, but dangerous leader. These folks can also be too opinionated and self-destructive, and have to hit bottom or confront a moral crisis before they can rise to higher levels of consciousness. They have the ability to make it in the material world, though, maybe more than people with many other placements of this planet.

Neptune in the Twelfth House

These natives possess grace, natural beauty, talent, an affinity for the arts, and a magical charisma. Yet they also have a tendency toward loneliness, perhaps because they feel they are superior to the masses, feeling special inside but not acting arrogant outwardly—just keeping the riffraff at arm's length. Paradoxically, they also have sympathy for and wish to help those in need—perhaps just from a distance.

A carefully selected lover and a few close friends may penetrate their elusiveness.

Here is another placement where the individual finds it hard to "get out of the starting gate." Prone to musings on the more esoteric, philosophical aspects of life (and death), a Twelfth-House Neptune gives unusual spiritual insight and psychic abilities.

Pluto in the Twelfth House

Pluto is a real pressure cooker. Discovered in the early 1930s, the outermost planet seemed to usher in unprecedented world events—Stalin's purges, the rise of Hitler, World War II, and the nuclear age. Plutonian energy resonates with atomic, volcanic power. When, where, and how it sits in a person's chart indicates powerful and potentially destructive tendencies.

The gurus say the Twelfth House, with its "backstage" aura, is then a fairly good place for this old troublemaker. Pluto is above the horizon, where its power can be harnessed in service, especially in large institutions such as hospitals and prisons. Folks with a Twelfth-House Pluto may not play by the rules or may prefer to work alone, but work they most definitely will.

These individuals have incredible drive and focus, and may also have the support of a sympathetic family.

If one can take orders and believe in a cause, this is a good placement for someone in, say, military Special Forces or covert operations. People with a Twelfth-House Pluto can get used to a Spartan lifestyle; they have the single-mindedness and also the self-discipline to immerse themselves in a difficult regimen that requires sacrifice and long periods of isolation.

Monks can have Pluto here too.

---

1. This is a common attribution to Cayce, and one of the slogans of the Association for Research and Enlightenment (A.R.E.) in Virginia Beach, Virginia. See http://www.edgarcayce.org.

2. Dana Gerhardt, "In Wonderland: The 12th House in Your Chart," *InnerSelf*, http://www.innerself.com.

3. "President-elect Lincoln survived an assassination attempt in Baltimore, and on February 23, 1861, arrived secretly in disguise to Washington, D.C. The South ridiculed Lincoln for this seemingly cowardly act, but the efforts at security may have been prudent." From the online site *U-S-History.com*, http://www.u-s-history.com/pages/h837.html.

CHAPTER SIXTEEN

Case Studies

Case Study 1: John
"The only one who could ever reach me, was the son of a preacher man."
—Dusty Springfield

They say redheads feel more pain than their fellow human beings, and I could see this applying to my russet-haired friend John. He had a vexing combination of toughness and tenderness, anger and sweetness. His Saturn in the Tenth House unconsciously drove him to succeed and "be a man in a man's world," but the planet was also retrograde, which compromises a person's defenses, making the individual extrasensitive. In fact, it sometimes feels as though there's no protection out there at all. This, combined with the Pisces Moon and the Libran Mars, just didn't make for a tough guy. John's nature was to be charming, to catch more flies with honey than with vinegar.

Then why in the heck did he join the Marines Corps, right in the middle of the Vietnam War? It was a decision that I greatly respect—considering the discipline, strength, and courage needed just to get through boot camp—but one that would lead to a devastating, life-altering injury.

I think the Tenth-House Saturn made him do it—he was trying to prove himself to a kind but often absent father.

Saturn here indicates those who have special concerns related to their father, as well as supervisors and other authority figures in general. These individuals may be separated at a young age from their father, or the father may be austere, strict, or overburdened with responsibilities.

John's father was a theologian, a leader in one of the large churches of our nation, and he frequently traveled nationally and internationally as a spiritual ambassador. I remember John telling me that, in fact, both of his parents were away a lot and he spent quite a bit of time as a young child living with his grandparents. He adored his "Nanny" and "Pop-pop," but even the most loving elders can't match the secure feeling parents give a little one.

They were also from a generation where the man of the house didn't participate much in child-rearing. It was that old-fashioned idea that it was the woman's job to raise the children and the man's job to put food on the table. So John didn't get as much masculine guidance and discipline from his grandfather as he would have from his own father.

And, indeed, I heard many stories of John being a holy terror—climbing the water tower in Lancaster, hiding near the bus stop with a water gun, squirting people when they got off the bus, celebrating the end of the school year by throwing stones and breaking every window in a factory (he said he thought it was abandoned). He was the quintessential mischievous "P. K."—preacher's kid.

Then, just on the cusp of adulthood, John joined the Marines, jumped feet first into the most macho group of guys you could find. And father figures abounded, from the drill sergeants to the legendary Commandant "Chesty" Puller, whom John said was saluted as the guys went to sleep each night.

The Corps may have helped him absorb the discipline he didn't get as a child. John might have truly been on his way to a higher level of self-respect, a feeling of accomplishment. But then he was terribly injured, and his life took a painful detour.

Fortunately, he was only nineteen, and youthful resilience helped him mend physically, but there were many inner scars that never healed.

Fast-forward about thirty years—past two marriages, a number of jobs, a lot of good times, and a couple of cross-country moves—and this is where I met John. Around the

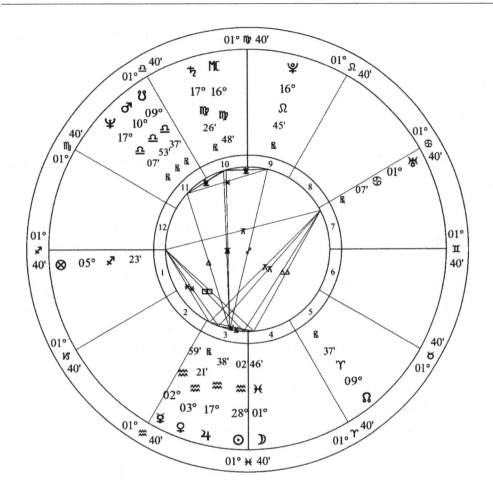

John
February 17, 1950 / 1:30 a.m. Standard Time
Time Zone: 5 hours West
Lancaster, PA / Equal Houses

time Starbucks started to go national, he was managing a chic little coffee shop in Philadelphia and dreaming of having his own place.

All those planets in Aquarius, as well as a stellium in the Eleventh House, gave him the desire to make money in an independent way, through his own efforts rather than working for a boss. For a brief period, he achieved his goal and had a coffee shop, but struggled to stay afloat. He had already started to come emotionally undone and was torn between the early-morning responsibilities of the shop and the allure of late-night partying. He managed for a while, but then his lack of discipline and groundedness (all those planets in air signs) took over.

Financial problems caused him to bring a partner onboard, a mismatch from the start. The partner had a completely separate business of his own and did little of the day-to-day running of the shop, yet assumed a superior position because of his experience. At first John spoke of him in glowing terms—there he was again, looking for a father figure (Tenth-House Saturn) to guide him, to help him make his way in the world. But the partner would just come in at the end of the day, take most of the receipts, give orders, and leave. John's "mentor" became just another authority figure whom he came to resent.

Sadly, less than a year after he opened his long-dreamed-of business, John closed it down. Then he really started to unravel.

Doctors and psychologists might say that what got him at the end was a combination of posttraumatic stress disorder, survivor's guilt, and real physical pain. But I think there was something spiritual lacking—he had become bereft of hope and lost faith in the material and ethereal worlds. The coffee shop was supposed to be the anchor that would steer John. When that didn't work out, I don't think he knew where to turn for a steady presence.

Just fifty at the time, John was looking down the road at his own mortality and felt he wouldn't have another chance. He had internalized a sense of failure, of not making it in the material world, which is so important to those with a Tenth-House Saturn. He hinted that he saw only ill health, pain, financial troubles, and isolation in the future.

Without the steady, loving guidance of a father early in childhood, people with a Tenth-House Saturn will often feel a sense of inadequacy, of being unable to stand on their own in society. I think this lack of confidence is especially present with men. Despite the advances of society in terms of understanding equality between the sexes, many men still need to feel, well, manly. And in our culture, a lot of this has to do with tangible success, achievement in the material world. For men with a Tenth-House Saturn, so close to the Midheaven, this need is even more powerful.

John also became obsessed with the fact that his father had passed away at the young age of fifty-two. He really bought into the idea that his time was near, too. Unfortunately, when you repeat a belief to yourself, you kind of create the reality—you make it a self-fulfilling prophecy.

My heart went out to him again and again. I never stopped believing in his good qualities and possibilities. But he had convinced himself that life was almost over.

John started to skip his therapy sessions at the veterans hospital and became negligent with his medication. If I wasn't there to drive him over to the hospital, he just wouldn't go. To make matters worse, one of his friends had a problem with substance abuse, which spilled over into John's life when he would invite John to party with him. People with the Moon in Pisces, who possess some very wonderful qualities, can also be susceptible to drug and alcohol abuse.

Toward the end, John told me he couldn't sleep and was having nightmares, even hallucinations. We can see in his chart that the man had almost all air and fire signs—he needed to be grounded in reality, not drifting off in a cloud of anodynes. It's interesting that Neptune, Mars, and the South Node are in his Eleventh House, the house of groups and attachments outside of the family. John had made a family out of his fellow partiers. Neptune nearly conjunct Mars in Libra means there's an element of fantasy, of cloudedness and denial. I'm sure deep down inside he knew he was self-destructing, but was probably in too deep to stop.

In addition, his friend was quite wealthy, and John just loved hanging around, digging his expensive car, stereo equipment, and "toys." Venus and Mercury are very close to the Second House (using the Tropical system, they actually are in the Second House), and John was turned on by the beautiful things the Second House represents—interior design, elegant clothes, expensive jewelry, fine food, and drink.

With Sagittarius rising, John worshiped mobility and freedom. Indeed, the friend certainly had this in abundance. The friend occasionally worked hard, but seemed to have huge blocks of free time, which also appealed to John's Sagittarius Ascendant—no tied-to-the-desk jobs in cubicle wonderland for him. He liked the freewheeling freelance life of his friend and of others in his milieu who had family money or businesses and professions that frequently took them across the globe.

My airy friend needed less flitting around to clubs and fancy restaurants and more activities like meditation, yoga, or simply walking, to balance the tendency toward flights of fancy and impracticality.

With an inquisitive mind (Mercury, Sun, and Jupiter in Aquarius, all in the Third House), John was well-read and well informed about news and current events, and loved to sit in cafes and drink espresso, *New York Times* in hand. But all that air gave him retention problems, which I think had plagued him since childhood. He enjoyed leaping from subject to subject, with little time to thoroughly mull over or digest what was being discussed. So when a difficult topic—like his emotional problems or his money problems—came up, we'd never really get to the heart of the matter.

He absolutely needed a stable environment or routine (Tenth-House Saturn) to calm his sensitive nervous system. (And all those espressos probably didn't help.) When the nerves took over, the demons would really haunt him.

And I do believe they were demons. Although I don't believe in Satan and I abhor black magic, dark forces do exist. When we allow our protective spirit—our connection to the light forces and angels—to be compromised, the demons can get in and really do a number on the soul and psyche. Some of this is chemical, of course. From a medical standpoint, there are chemical imbalances and misfiring synapses that lead to mental illness—and can thankfully be treated with medication.

But I have also read theories that say recreational drugs and too much alcohol—along with improper thinking and behavior—can contaminate or break down our aura of protection, our connection to the light. I recall once sitting with John and trying to give him Reiki, laying my hands on the curly red hair that covered his head, trying to be gentle because of the scars on his scalp from the war injuries there. It was like sparks were coming out of the crown-chakra area. Honestly, it felt like static electricity was coursing from his head into my hands. He was *wired*. No wonder he was using various substances to quiet his mind.

I began to wonder if something on a supernatural level had happened to John. In the last six months of his life, his personality changed so much. The charming, sensitive, kind, funny man turned dark. Mean, bitter, ugly words came out of his mouth, and he would get angry and dictatorial. That's the darkest side of Saturn in the Tenth House.

I could also see that he was becoming more disheveled, and his clothes and apartment were increasingly filthy, the lovely things and collection of CDs scattered on the floor or broken. All of this was way out of character for him, and it quickly grew beyond anything I could help with. And when I tried to be kind, out came those abusive remarks. To preserve my sanity, and at the suggestions of friends, his parents, and a number of self-help books, I withdrew, just occasionally sending an encouraging card or leaving a phone message. He never seemed to be home anyway.

The idea was to let him "hit bottom," which sounds cruel. According to everyone I spoke with, this was the most humane thing to do. We couldn't stop him from abusing himself—he was the only one who could make that choice.

In fact, John tried to commit suicide in the early summer. I went to see him—I had to—and cried when I saw the scars on his wrists. Thank God he had cut himself the wrong way, so the bleeding hadn't been too bad. But what had happened to my brilliant friend? Who or what was inside his heart driving him to destruction?

We all thought that was "the bottom" he was supposed to hit. Unfortunately, I, his "healthy" friends and neighbors, and his parents all were wrong.

I saw him one last time, in mid-August 2001, and had a terrible meeting. He was dressed in dirty clothes, just a hair away from looking like a homeless person. He hadn't shaved, and his rough beard and angry demeanor gave him a threatening look. With his red hair and beard, he looked like he was playing an Irish madman in a movie.

And he was so mean. Everything I said—even "Are you all right?"—seemed to be fightin' words. The afternoon ended at a coffee house—always with the coffee!—and with me in tears. I had to walk away from him. He yelled stuff as I left, and followed up with some scathing e-mails. I thought that was about the worst thing that was going to happen that year. Little did I know.

I got one last e-mail from John, implying that he was leaving the area, perhaps to go to Norfolk, Virginia, with its big Navy presence and support system for veterans. I encouraged him to do so, to get away from Philly and start anew, and to please be well and know that I still loved him.

"I'm outta here," was the last thing he wrote.

Over the Labor Day weekend, there was a full moon, and I spent a lonely evening outdoors in meditation and contemplation of the cycles of the Earth, the passing of time. Listening to the crickets and cicadas, I knew summer was almost over. Deep in meditation that night, I felt a heaviness in my chest, a profound sadness that moved me to tears. I couldn't stop crying, and I didn't know why. Something had just really touched me. I thought about John.

A little more than a week later, as I watched the news coverage of the September 11, 2001, attacks on New York and Washington, I shook with emotion, fear, disbelief, and sadness. Who could I talk to about this, to kick around all the thoughts and feelings we all were dealing with? My natural ally on such subject matters was John, since he was so well-read and enjoyed these types of discussions. In his fragile state, I also hoped this tragedy wasn't upsetting him even more. I broke my promise to my friends and called him, but there was no answer.

I believe he was already dead.

I later learned that neighbors had found him lifeless on his bathroom floor. Everyone suspected an overdose, although the official cause of death was heart attack. I didn't know this until a few weeks later, when his family called me to break the news. I imagine that the TV was probably on, as it always was, broadcasting the terrible news of September 11 as he lay there. Thank goodness he was spared from that horror.

However he had died, the long, painful march was over. He was finally at peace.

Then I remembered the e-mail message "I'm outta here" and the deep, grieving presence I had felt during meditation. Had John passed over that very night? Was it his soul "visiting" me, saying goodbye? It was so utterly mournful, like a spirit boat overloaded with the weight of demons.

After John's funeral, for months and even years, I kept finding notes and long letters he had handwritten to me. With the Sun and Jupiter in his Third House, he loved to communicate, and he would frequently surprise me with a letter, stuck under my door or on my windshield. I was torn as to whether I should throw them away or save them to help me remember the generous, kind, and loving side of John, the part of the man I fell for and what I truly believe was at the core of his being.

I've read that Kurt Vonnegut said to never throw away your old love letters, and indeed, I decided to keep the cards and things tucked away in a shoebox. When I touch the paper and run my fingers over the unusual handwriting, I can remember the good times we had and the positive things John brought to my life. That's what I'd like to think about.

I hope that wherever his soul travels, it is passing through the cosmos lightened of its burden. If anyone deserves to heal and resolve his karma, and reincarnate into a joyful life filled with light and laughter, it's my friend.

Case Study 2: Gwyneth Bryan

I thought a tour of the hot spots around my own chart, guided by my reflections, years of inner work, and the knowledge that comes with middle age, might be enlightening. I hope this will provide some real insight for folks who share similar placement of planets within the houses, or angles between certain planets.

The Challenges

I'd like to start with my Third House, which contains a powerful grouping of planets, including the Moon, Neptune, and Jupiter. I will also talk about the connection between this house and my many planets in the Twelfth House, the house of karma, mysticism, secrets, and healing. There are several squares between the Third- and Twelfth-House planets, which have brought challenges, friction, and life lessons.

The Third House describes one's mental state, intellectual orientation, self-expression, and communications, as well as early education, immediate environment (such as your neighborhood), and encounters with siblings and cousins. Neptune in the Third House indicates skill in writing, and indeed I seem to have found my groove with writing and reporting. This dreamy, idealistic planet has also led me in a search for a kind of perfection and bliss in the world, which has sometimes also brought disappointments, especially with people.

I, and others with this placement, tend to idealize others and may be overly trusting in a world where, unfortunately, people tend to be out for themselves. If you're like me, perhaps you have been taken advantage of, or have been expected to "rescue" others.

In addition, I live between New York and Philadelphia, and this is no place to be an unquestioning flower child. When I lived in the city, I could never quite comprehend the loutish behavior of certain people, and how competitive others could be. But that's the city for you—survival of the fittest. People with Neptune in the Third might, in general, be better off living outside of an urban area. I know I have less anxiety in smaller towns.

If you must be in the city, though, how to deal? Employing the more positive aspects of Neptune in the Third House, I will digress a little and talk about a spiritual approach to handling a world that frequently seems harsh and punishing. I belong to a study group organized by the Association for Research and Enlightenment (the A.R.E./Edgar Cayce Society), and we often talk about how a person working toward higher understanding should try to act when confronted with ignorance.

As Cayce, and many other "masters" and guides have agreed, the bottom line is always love, and the ultimate enlightenment comes when we realize that we are all one, we are all of the light. You see that the person who is behaving badly is just another "piece" of the light, of God, and may indeed just be a reflection of a negative aspect of yourself. Or, the person might be vibrating on a lower level, simply not conscious of his or her behavior. James, the co-facilitator of our group, calls people who act out or act selfishly "walking opportunities"—in other words, they provide an opportunity for us to take what we have learned and physically employ it. Sure, it's easy to live a spiritual, peaceful life in a community filled with like-minded people, but the real challenge is to get out there and stay positive when people are butting in front of you in line, interrupting or insulting you, or generally being rude or unkind.

If we are centered and remain aware of the presence of the light within ourselves, we can walk comfortably among difficult people, places, and circumstances. Perhaps they might even learn from our example. A friend pointed out that truly enlightened individuals, such as Mother Teresa, can live among the sick and not fall ill themselves because they're vibrating at such an advanced level that they are impervious to earthly negativity.

Perhaps I will be there someday, but it got to be a bit much for me in the city. I think the last straw was when people started shooting each other for taking their parking spaces.

After living in a tough-guy town like Philly for about ten years, I needed a more peaceful place of residence. I moved north, to an old colonial town dotted with preserved farmland, and immediately felt the lighter, cleaner energy. Right now, I can hear songbirds coming from the tree line that separates my backyard from a farmer's field, and my cats are wandering in and out of the front door, which I have propped ajar. (Never in the city would I do that!) It's so different from the sounds of the city—construction vehicles, police and EMT sirens, and people shouting and swearing.

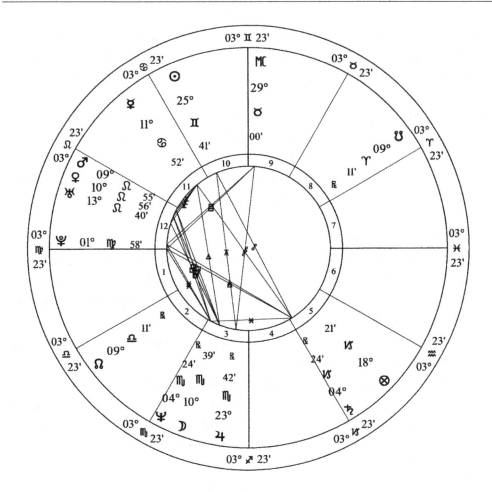

Gwyneth Bryan

I might suggest to others with Neptune in the Third House that, if their astonishing sensitivity is being tested by the low, injurious vibrations found in cities, they consider a move. It might mean readjusting their lifestyle (usually you don't make as much money away from urban centers), but it could be lifesaving in terms of physical and mental health.

Also, having Neptune and the Moon in the Third House indicates that living near or spending time by the sea is healing for the individual. That truly resonates for me. I have always loved the ocean and am energized by it. As far as settling down and retiring, the Pacific Coast north of San Francisco, the Gulf Coast of Florida, the Florida Keys, or Hawaii would be quite nice, as I've told my husband many times!

Communications Breakdown

All these planets in the natural house of communications should make me an easy conversationalist, a natural-born teacher, maybe even a bit of a blabbermouth (Jupiter in the Third), but I have always had issues with communication, especially verbal communication. I have frequently had to fight to keep from being overwhelmed—in certain cases, from being completely ignored—by others who are more talkative and aggressive. (Virgo rising also indicates a rather shy person.)

The position of Neptune in a person's chart indicates special, intuitive talents in that area, but also points to a certain cloudiness and naïveté in dealing with those issues. This planet, as well as the Moon and Jupiter, are in my Third House, and the sign on the cusp is Scorpio, so there's tremendous, sometimes overwhelming intensity tied up with all of this "wanting to be heard."

For me, I have always felt that there was passion behind what I wanted to say, but perhaps because of all those squares with the Twelfth House, I ended up being kind of stifled from properly expressing myself, until I was almost boiling inside and the words came out in inappropriate ways. Where did this come from?

I was born with strong, sometimes raw feelings (Moon in Scorpio). In contrast, I have been told that I was a fairly quiet baby—but my early childhood, especially in school, was difficult. At times a little shy and overly sensitive around the other kids (Moon conjunct Neptune)—who could be pretty cruel, truth be told—I guess I expressed my displeasure too often. I remember feeling a lot of injustice, so I cried a lot, which didn't win me any popularity points. Remember when kids used to get graded on their behavior? I got a "U" (unsatisfactory) in "exercises self-control" and "works and plays well with others." This was long before the idea of promoting self-esteem took hold in public schools. You could get failing grades for your personality! And, of course, there were no school psychologists to step in and offer suggestions (like maybe I needed to go to a school with other more sensitive, creative types).

Home life was also challenging. My parents, both Scorpios, were very intense and would sometimes have ripsnorting arguments. When Scorpios do anything, they do it to the max. I want to say that they were also affectionate to each other and us, and they certainly mellowed with age. But when they were younger, they sure let everyone know when they were mad!

I would try to find a cozy corner, or my sister would put her arm around me and we'd ride out the storm. But it frightened me. As a child, I didn't know why they were shouting, and sometimes I worried that I'd done something wrong. And I also worried that they were going to get a divorce.

I thought that being quiet would help keep the peace. But still, there was this volatile energy that, with my great sensitivity, I couldn't help but feel and absorb.

Now that I have lived to middle age and have had my own ups and downs, I can better understand my mom, and why some of these arguments occurred. She was fighting for her freedom, her individuality, her rights as a person. Like many gals from her generation (before women's liberation), marriage and children meant putting dreams aside and putting herself in a little box society created—and taking on very adult, role-bound responsibilities, often just out of college, even high school. Today, by contrast, adolescence can last as long as age thirty, and there are many more choices for young women, so these heavy responsibilities are postponed.

My mom had a lively personality and had had a nice career in teaching before staying home to raise us. I think she was frustrated being at home in a small town with only two little children as company, waiting on my rather old-fashioned father.

As was very common back then, she was there to wait on him and raise children, and she was discouraged from thinking about being involved in teaching again or doing much of anything in the outside world. Although many of the women in our neighborhood had jobs outside the home, to help with the household income if not to pursue a career, my mom stayed home. And, in retrospect, she worked like a horse.

When we moved in with Dad for a while at the end of his life, I used to shake my head and wonder how any woman could live like Mom and many women of her generation used to (and, probably, women of a certain income bracket still do). I never worked so hard in my life. As soon as the breakfast was done and cleaned up, it was time for lunch, and as soon as that was over, I had to start thinking about dinner—plus grocery shopping, laundry, and house cleaning. Any stay-at-home mom can relate to this. And I was taking care of only my dad—I can't imagine dealing with little children as well. I tip my hat to you ladies with little ones, but I couldn't wait to get back to my job!

See, I now know why Mom and Dad would sometimes erupt. My mom was understandably frustrated by the lack of freedom to express her creativity, and she was probably just plain tired from all the work. Again, I wondered how much better things would have been with family therapy or marriage counseling. But back then, psychology was "only for crazy people."

Happily, after my sister and I were fairly grown, we suggested Mom take a job at an upscale retail clothing store, where she became revitalized. After a move to another store with even more beautiful items, she became a top salesperson, making a tidy sum from commissions and nurturing her younger colleagues.

Back at home, as a child, when things became heated, my coping strategy was to try to stay quiet. "Maybe if I do everything perfectly, don't rock the boat, and say nothing, things will get better," I'd think to myself.

I think that's where some of the communication blockage that still plagues me was put into place. I was conditioned to "keep the lid on," even if my feelings were overwhelming. I absorbed the message that I was supposed to inhibit my self-expression.

This is the kind of karma people with squared or challenged Third Houses might encounter. To this day, I am learning techniques for assertiveness, how to express my rights as a person. Through cognitive behavioral therapy I have learned to filter my illusions (Neptune) about what people might mean when we interact, then step back and logically understand my feelings (Moon) before I react. The memories of a childhood with locked-up feelings and an inability to properly express them could have led to a lifetime of being unable to communicate with others. And I still struggle with speaking my truth. But I also have worked hard and found new, creative ways to express myself—writing and journaling, for example. Perhaps this could work for you too.

This placement of the Moon in the Third House, when progressed to midlife, has also brought lessons of creating and maintaining emotional boundaries with family, peers, and romantic partners. The Moon is a watery body and is connected with fluid boundaries, so it frequently brings up questions concerning healthy emotional and psychic boundaries with others. The Moon also signifies nurturing archetypes, and the Third House symbolizes equal relationships. At midlife, as I have experienced, it is most necessary for me to establish fair and equal partnerships. I am done with the domineering, one-sided relationships I have experienced with some romantic partners, coworkers, and relatives. If others have not honored my articulated desire for equality, I have had to put distance between us, so some relationships have fallen apart.

Perhaps others with a similar placement of the Moon and Neptune have experienced being used, being dominated, or always having to rescue others. These various forms of codependence keep such people from growing themselves, understanding their soul's purpose, and working toward higher consciousness. So it's good, especially at midlife, to take a look and see if these issues are holding you back from enjoying more satisfying relationships as well as putting more energy into your own growth and awareness—and, as I have done with writing and journaling, taking the energy of the Third House and directing it in a positive way. Blending communication with creativity is a healthy way to work through these sometimes paradoxical energies.

The Physical Manifestations of Communications Breakdown

I am greatly interested in the mind-body connection and am a great fan of such thinkers and writers as Caroline Myss, Deepak Chopra, and Louise Hay, who say, essentially, that all illness is manifested by improper thinking, by negative attitudes—by the mind.

This is why open communications, properly expressing one's emotions, is so very important. Those with communications and Third-House challenges—or whose Sun, Moon, or Ascendant is in Gemini—might be plagued with throat, esophagus, mouth, teeth, neck, and shoulder problems. As one intuitive healer told me, a stiff neck, shoulder knots, hoarseness, and such issues as stuttering or dyslexia indicate an improper flow of energy between the head and the heart.

"If the mind and heart are not communicating clearly with each other, one will dominate the other," writes Myss in her book *Anatomy of the Spirit*. "When our minds are in the lead, we suffer emotionally because we turn emotional data into an enemy. We seek to control all situations and relationships and maintain authority over emotions. When our hearts are in the lead, we tend to maintain the illusion that all is well. Whether the mind is in the lead or the heart, will is motivated by fear and the futile goal of control, not by an internal sense of security."[1]

I certainly have endured years of neck pain, helped by chiropractic care, ice and heat packs, massage—and aspirin. The source of this injury and pain is mysterious—I was in a minor car accident when young, but I don't think I got whiplash. Chiropractors sometimes say it can go all the way back to birth, when the doctor twists a baby's neck to coax it from the birth canal. Or, it could be karmic—an injury I sustained in a previous life has come back to haunt me in this incarnation.

Indeed, a shamanic healer recently told me the amazing story as she chanted and prayed over this knot in my upper neck, which has seemingly been there forever. She said the information she was receiving indicated that I was a man in a frontier town in a previous life, and I had accidentally been sprayed with birdshot, a piece of which lodged just below my right ear. (Ironically, I had this session the same week Vice President Dick Cheney shot one of his buddies while quail hunting.)

The nerve damage caused great pain and, unfortunately, a speech impediment. I went through life mumbling and coercing words from my mouth, becoming more and more bitter, and eventually putting a wall around my heart to keep other people away. I couldn't deal with the ridicule of being the "cripple" or the "retard" in town. You know how cruel provincial people can be. What they didn't realize was that I had a good mind and a talent for writing, even though I sounded like Gabby Hayes. The healer told me I had found work on a frontier newspaper, and these written communication skills carried over into this lifetime.

Unfortunately, so did the occasional difficulties with being properly heard and respected by others.

But I also lean toward the idea that, like many women of my generation, and as mentioned before, I was conditioned to "be nice," to button my lip if something displeased me, or if I did object, to couch my words politely. And, except in rare circumstances, I have been discouraged from addressing the very deepest thoughts from my heart and soul. Thank God for the few personal places where I can speak from the heart. But in polite society, in public, in the workplace, and in many families, this is not allowed. That's not uncommon, though.

In a society and culture of sound bytes and sitcom ripostes, there are many, many people unable to express what is in their hearts. We are discouraged from soul-searching, from digging deep and expressing our most profound truths. Even a presidential speech is filled with buzz words and expressions, written to push the buttons of a mass audience. It might have been different when leaders like Lincoln were also writers and thinkers and could stir listeners with their words because they themselves were searching their souls, but those days are gone forever. Now we have pop-culture catch phrases to express our tribal consciousness.

Keeping all this in mind, for individuals with Neptune, the Moon, or several planets in the Third House, especially if they are aspected rather poorly, it is essential to learn how to speak our truth, to connect the heart, mind, thought, word, and action. This affects the areas of the body previously mentioned, but spirals throughout our whole being to affect our spiritual growth as well.

Healing Blocked Communication/Fifth Chakra

Healing the fifth chakra, which is ruled by Mercury (which rules Gemini and is therefore naturally connected to the Third House), is imperative if we want to open to the intuitive awareness that comes from the sixth and seventh chakras. If the fifth chakra is blocked, we may be overly mental and not open to the subtle intuitive information that is constantly being channeled through the higher centers. In terms of healing modalities, singing is one of the best methods for opening the fifth chakra.

Since many people with fifth-chakra blockages have literally "lost their voice," one of the best ways to reclaim one's voice is to vibrate it with sound.

Just today I realized that I used to sing all the time, but I rarely, if ever, sing now. (By the way, parents, if you notice a child bursting with song and possessing an ability to carry a decent tune and remember complex words, you might have an individual on your hands who was a performer in a previous life. Don't quash this little one's talent.)

Ironically, when I didn't know what I was doing, the music flowed through me so organically. And even in high school we had some direction, but the emphasis was still on fun, not perfection or competition. That changed when I went to college to actually study music. (More about this later when we talk about the Fifth House in my chart.)

You couldn't just open your mouth and sing—there had to be perfect pronunciation, pitch, and timbre. Even the choirs were sober ensembles that took themselves very seriously. And everyone was so straight and repressed. Where was the joy of just singing?

I went back to making a joyful noise in the car and the shower, but even that tapered off. I'm not sure why. Perhaps it was due to aging, absorbing the idea that we have to become more subdued as we grow older, or to sitting in a rather emotionally repressed office, where the organizational, thinking side of the brain is the only part that is activated.

An intuitive healer recommended that I try again to just sing from the heart. She suggested, if I couldn't actually sing songs, to "tone" various syllables and mantras—"love," "OM," "peace," or even my name. And it helped, although I still prefer a nice Cole Porter tune.

I also had a chance to sing a little at a cousin's wedding, just spiritual songs from the hymnal. But it was a joy to make music, to breathe deeply through the notes and phrases and read music again.

Kirtan chanting was also a profound experience for me and might help others with a blocked or challenged Third House. Essentially the repetition of syllables and bits and pieces of sacred Sanskrit text, you gather in a group and just sing and tone for an hour or more, accompanied by minimal instruments, maybe just guitar and harmonium and hand drums. I didn't even know what I was singing, but I could feel the essence of the words and the sentiment. Because there's group energy involved, an evening of kirtan chant is almost like a massive prayer session.

By the end of the evening, during one very touching piece, tears flowed from my eyes and I felt a tingle up my spine—an indication that my heart chakra had opened and I was touching a little bit of mystery, light, God. I felt lighter and more at peace when it was over, and I hope sincerely to do more.

Other ways to work with healing the fifth chakra, and therefore issues with the Third House, is to meditate on a light-blue color, like robin's-egg blue. Or wear this color, in a dress, blouse, sweater, or scarf—something that touches your throat area. Special stones and crystals, especially turquoise (the master healer) and lapis lazuli, are good for working with this chakra. Wear a necklace, dangle a pair of earrings with these stones, or carry them with you for healing energy.

The Blessings

With the Moon and Neptune conjunct, and trine to Mercury in the Eleventh House, I am able to convey complex subject matters, and my college papers on metaphysics, mysticism, and philosophy were frequently praised by my teachers. This also taps into the Twelfth House—and my fascination with such material.

The "friction" or energy generated between my Third- and Twelfth-House planets gives me a kind of determination to "get that information out there" and to communicate, no matter what. This configuration may not make me a social butterfly or the life of the party. Instead, I focus on touching the deepest depths of human experience, through psychology, intuitive experiences, spirituality, and healing. My sincere desire is to bring this information to others through writing.

I recall a course in mysticism and the paranormal that turned me on to a number of seekers, authors, and thinkers whose ideas have stayed with me to this day. In that class we perused the Seth material, focused on Zen Buddhism with The Empty Mirror, and most profoundly for me, studied Gina Cerminara's book about Edgar Cayce, *Many Mansions*. That book, expounding on Cayce's work with reincarnation and karma, fascinated me.

I just drank it up, like a person who had been thirsty for knowledge for years. And, in fact, like a missing piece to a puzzle, it changed my philosophy about what happens after we die. I believe this was a bit of enlightenment, and it was a huge step on the longer road to raising my awareness and vibrational level.

A few years after leaving college, I found a Cayce study group nearby and experienced more lessons and powerful information, and also met some extraordinary people and forged lasting friendships. A couple of relocations took me away from that great fellowship, but just recently I have been involved with another study group, providing a rare place for me to communicate (Third House) about my passion for spiritual knowledge (Twelfth House). Tying the Third and Twelfth Houses together, I wrote a feature story for a New Age magazine praising the concept of the study groups and sharing some of the wisdom—and fun—that comes from this fellowship.

Lately, I've also noticed that whenever something "New Agey" comes to the office where I work (a course in finding your animal spirit, for example), my editor hands it to me. My colleagues kind of chuckle ("There's another Gwyn story"), but I dive right in, enjoying the conversations and food for thought. I also hope that by publishing such articles, and getting the material out there to the general public, that this is serving humanity and helping to heal the planet, in a way. The more the mainstream considers the various roads to inner knowledge and peace, perhaps the more we can fight the negativity and brutality that seem to be consuming our species.

I'm a public relations person (Third House) for spiritual awareness and healing (Twelfth House). See, it is possible to overcome the kinds of challenges several squares in a chart can throw. I think it was astrologer Debbi Kempton-Smith who described folks with squares and oppositions in their charts as having tough lives, but being more interesting than people with nothing but trines and sunshine in their birth horoscopes.

Plus, as I've remarked before, the chart is a blueprint for one's personality, but just as a building can be modified, so can the rough spots in this "blueprint." Your will is always the most powerful factor in how your life turns out.

Third House and Creative Writing

The Moon in the Third, like the Moon in Gemini, indeed points to people who were born to communicate, cajole, and catalogue stories about themselves and the people they know, as they love to observe human beings and their foibles. They also love to interject themselves into their writing and works of art. Think of writers such as Jay McInerney, whose novels, like *Bright Lights, Big City* and *The Good Life*, contain characters whose personalities and chic circumstances are very much like the personalities and chic circumstances of Jay McInerney and his circle of friends.

Ernest Hemingway (Jupiter in the Third House, late in Libra) was another author who famously observed and listened to his friends, family, fellow authors, and drinking buddies, and drew upon their personality traits and physical characteristics, weaving this information into his novels and short stories. The gnarled hands of the fisherman in *The Old Man and the Sea* were taken from his real-life mate on the Pilar, for example. It is said that Hemingway's afternoons and evenings at Sloppy Joe's and other watering holes in Key West were like journalistic, story-gathering expeditions.

He would hunker down with the various characters, everyone getting well lubricated and sharing their yarns, and then recount those stories and voices when he sat down to write the following day. Even after consuming a respectable quantity of alcohol, he could recall these conversations almost verbatim, and he had a genius of an ear for hearing and recollecting colorful language, speech, and colloquialisms. He was able to work this into his dialogue, which is one of the things that makes his fiction come alive and seem so real.

Not that I'm a great writer who can weave stories of my friends and family into literature. But I write best when I can include something I have experienced. I also use anecdotes and personal experience when I counsel someone in astrology or tarot. I often remember friends or family with similar charts and try to use this information to be helpful to my clients, or I can recall a circumstance when I was experiencing something similar, and then describe some techniques I used to work through the problem.

This all works very well and comes out with fluidity when I have the opportunity to write down my thoughts, or if I have the attention of one or two people, such as in a counseling session—or with very intimate friends.

But having my say in groups has been a lifelong challenge, and I attribute that to the squares to the Third-House Moon and Neptune, as well as my Moon being ruled by Scorpio. I like deep, meaningful talk with intelligent people. I founder in places where you have to make small talk. Here, I usually end up just nodding and laughing and seething as people talk over me.

With the more noisy, self-absorbed crowds, by the time I get the steam up to put my two cents in, usually the group conversation has moved on. Perhaps it's different in other parts of the country, but you have to speak very quickly and assertively around here (New York, New Jersey, and Philadelphia). I heard Garrison Keillor joke that if a New Yorker moved to Lake Wobegon, he would lose his voice from doing all the talking and arguing, because Minnesotans would just say, "Oh, I didn't know you felt that way. Hmmm."

With writing, though, there doesn't seem to be a problem with blockages. It's the same with my very best friends, e-mail correspondents, and fellow letter writers. It's just too bad that so many people these days are fast talkers and interrupters, and not too interested in hearing deeper thoughts or giving a person the space to put together a well-articulated sentence. (Who needs that when you can jump from subject to subject in three seconds flat? Gwyn, you're boring!)

This may be left over from the previous life as a "man of few words" on the frontier. Perhaps it took me too long to get the words out back then, and people had little patience but lots of ridicule.

Indeed, folks like me with challenges to the Third House may absorb the idea that "no one wants to listen to them," but I must emphasize that this is not true. No one should ever feel that they have nothing worthwhile to say! If there seems to be no outlet for expression, find a good therapist (they're paid to listen), join a book discussion group (usually a place that attracts thoughtful people), or check out Toastmasters, a group designed to give reticent people experience speaking in public.

Or, if you're not ready to go forth verbally, do what everyone else is doing: get on the Internet and put a blog together—you can say whatever you want!

But don't ever give up on expressing what you feel, speaking from the heart—having your say. It's your birthright to speak fully and freely.

Creative Challenges—Saturn in the Fifth House

Indeed, when we move on to look at the Fifth House in my chart, and the placement of Saturn there, it seems like the fates have conspired to keep me from creative expression. We touched on this a bit in the chapter about the Fifth House, but I would like to elaborate on my personal experience with this challenging placement, make some interesting connections, and offer some suggestions to those people who find Saturn in this space in their charts.

Here is a real potential for creative challenges and downright blocks for artists and performers. The Fifth House, ruled by Leo, is all about play, romance, luck, creativity, and children, whereas Saturn has to do with limitations, regimentation, life lessons, and karma.

Put these two together, and the spontaneity and joyfulness of the Fifth House are dampened by discipline, unlucky breaks, and delays. Some folks with Saturn in Leo might find so many stumbling blocks along the road to creative expression that they just give up or succumb to depression, a feeling that they just don't have it in them to create.

Never, never give up, though. We are all born creative and have the birthright and even the need to allow our playfulness and creative ideas to flow freely.

A valuable lesson—one that resonates with my own life story—is that this natural creativity is often schooled or conditioned out of us, by discouraging family members, school personnel, peer pressure, society, or the "legitimate work" we need to do to put a roof over our heads and food on the table. But those of us with this placement must never let that creative flame go out. There's always something that will showcase your special talents and artistry—cooking a fabulous dinner, decorating your house, adorning the Christmas tree, or even just the way you dress.

If actually making visual art, writing, playing music, or being in the theater isn't possible, look to other areas in life where you can exercise the inner, creative child.

Consider my story as a budding musician and sometimes actor. As I mentioned, I was fine—loved playing, loved singing and dancing—until I went to music school!

Here's what happened, and it's a very telling Saturn-in-the-Fifth-House story.

I had a lot of natural talent that just came bursting forth as a very young child. My friends and I were always putting on shows, turning the garage into a stage, with curtains and costume changes, and strutting showbiz-style down the driveway, cane in hand.

I had a good ear and could hear a song on the radio just a few times and pretty much get the music and words.

And, in my little world where everyone was doing so much talking, I learned to amuse myself by listening to the radio and records. So I knew all these Broadway songs you'd think only adults would know.

I would also put on a show for my biggest fan—my grandfather—sometimes even "dinner theater." We had a funny, special rapport, and it was a place for make-believe, away from the rest of the family, who kind of just ignored the "show" in the other room. I must have been obnoxious, quite frankly, but my grandfather was never critical and always gave me a big hand. In fact, sometimes I thought he was never going to stop clapping. (That was his sense of humor.) Then I'd launch into "my act."

You'd think that there was no creative block anywhere in my chart, looking back on this showbiz game we used to play. But, of course, when I grew up, peer pressure told me to cool it, so there were no more Broadway revues in the garage or private stagings for my grandfather.

My musical talents were channeled toward woodwind instruments and band, which was a thrill when I first got hold of the instrument (a clarinet) and saw how much I could learn and improve. That's the structure of Saturn in the Fifth House as we grow older. Organic play is discouraged, and in its place come goal-oriented, "proper" things, with more structure.

Even high school was fine, as I went through different peaks and plateaus, purchasing an instrument suitable for recitals and orchestral play, and taking lessons from more experienced teachers. I always loved the concerts, being part of a larger group that would sometimes really click.

Indeed, Saturn in the Fifth House does well as a part of a creative organization like an orchestra or symphonic band or choir. Conductors, with their ability to control and organize the group, epitomize Saturn in the Fifth House. I can imagine that members of a theatrical chorus line might fit into this category too. They're not in the spotlight, but their collective efforts are essential to an exciting production.

Anyway, I thought I was doing just fine with music.

Flash-forward to the conservatory of a small, Eastern liberal arts college.

Don't think for a moment that studying music at the conservatory level is lighthearted, fun, and easy. It was the most regimented, demanding schedule I'd ever experienced, and it was seven days a week, since we sometimes performed on the weekends and we were supposed to practice every day. I wonder how many other frustrated, overworked music majors had this heavy planet in the Fifth House.

It's a perfect metaphor for this placement: something as joyful and natural as music gets turned into a gerbil wheel of classes, group lessons on your instrument, group lessons on other instruments, private lessons, practice sessions, small and large ensemble work, homework, and planning recitals. The first year, I went from 8 a.m. to 8 p.m. on certain days, when rehearsals followed a day filled with classes. There was little time for socializing and, quite frankly, little time for actually enjoying or listening to music.

For a person with a different personality who has Saturn in the Fifth House, this might suit him or her fine. Indeed, creativity, when tinged with the Saturnian influence, often comes about through discipline and hard work. Mastering a musical instrument would be a very good example for this placement, as would becoming skilled as a photographer through printing techniques in the darkroom or with computer software. Printmakers—whom I call the "engineers of the art world"—would probably fall into this category as well.

However, my experience at the conservatory was to feel joyless, stressed, and just plain tired. And this was a liberal arts college—I can't imagine what a place like Juilliard would be like.

I suppose they were trying to weed out the serious musicians from the not-so-serious, and perhaps it got better for the upperclassmen. I just couldn't see going through this ordeal, and came to grips with the fact that I wasn't cut out for a career as a professional, where you sometimes practice for hours on end. (I thought practicing was incredibly lonely.) So I decided to change my major and degree program but still participate in some music activities.

I'm still thankful that I made that decision, because, from the outside looking in, I saw a whole lot of tense, unhappy-looking people. So repressed!

Sadly, after school was over, I rarely played my instrument, and twenty-five years on, I still haven't taken part in instrumental or vocal ensembles. That's Saturn in the Fifth House. For a long time, I took to heart that I wasn't good enough or disciplined enough, which is ridiculous when you consider that singing should just be opening your mouth and letting sound come out. Then life just got busy. I focused more on writing, and the time to play and sing just never materialized.

That's another thing that happens to people with Saturn in the Fifth House. They can become workaholics, putting so much energy into the workplace that creative outlets and play time are scheduled over. If this sounds like you, and you're longing to sing or play or be in a theater group again, it might be time to reassess your priorities. Can you find a slice of time in there to be creative? Can you take an occasional mental health day? Many people find themselves immersed in creative activities when they retire, but I hope our generation, so often tied to the desk, doesn't have to wait that long.

I have also considered the idea of karma, insofar as I didn't make it as a musician in this lifetime. Those who believe in reincarnation know we have many more opportunities to come back and try again, and all the good that we have done in this lifetime goes in the book and we pick it up and run next time around. People with a Fifth-House Saturn, who have an unfortunate propensity for doubting their talents, might take this to heart. Remember, nothing productive or educational is ever wasted as we continue to ride the karmic wheel.

Happily, the teachers, disciplinarians, and work requirements never totally pulled the plug on my music. I have never stopped listening to or following or exploring recorded music. And one of the happy side stories to my job reporting on the arts is that I often get to talk to musicians, who send me their new CDs, offer tickets to concerts, and so on. With my background, we can usually talk easily.

So for me, there are endless opportunities to love music, and that's what is ultimately most important. Sometimes I think my fellow students in that music department were working so hard that they forgot this.

Karma

In fact, upon reflection, karma has played a great role in structuring (Saturn) my creativity (Fifth House). In retrospect, there was really no meaningful place for me to go with music and theater. The stage was a fun hobby that I shared with eccentric, amusing theater people, but it would have only distracted me from more meaningful pursuits. Music had become a too-rigorous discipline, and once I got home from college, there were few if any outlets for performance. I knew enough about myself to realize that I didn't have the discipline, personality, or talent to be a professional. That led me to writing and immersing myself in studies of metaphysics, as well as counseling others through astrology and tarot.

This is Saturn in the Fifth House personified. Saturn is the Lord of Karma, and the area of the chart where this planet sits indicates that the individual will have to understand some kind of life lesson before the issues of the specific house can be understood or fulfilled.

For me, and others with a Fifth-House Saturn, we need to incorporate our creativity with our soul's purpose, link it up with what we came here to do in this incarnation. Saturn may limit playfulness and lightheartedness, but when steered in the proper direction, creativity will come to more than just an individual's self-expression. One's creative efforts will have more meaning, more purpose, on a scale that goes way beyond the personal. There might not be acknowledgement of the ego—in other words, the Saturn-in-the-Fifth person will work long and hard but may not receive the recognition others enjoy—but the individual might inspire others to heal, to seek higher awareness.

A person with a Fifth-House Saturn, especially in favorable aspect to other planets, could lead others "up the mountaintop." And this could actually be part of the reason the individual incarnated in this lifetime.

A person might kick against the kind of blockages and delays Saturn brings to artistic efforts and self-expression. But acknowledging the karmic ramifications of this placement lifts one beyond the need for ego gratification, and brings a much broader, planetary understanding. It's a more meaningful way to view this heavy planet in the house of play.

For me, I had to try acting, singing, and playing an instrument in my younger years, all things that brought pleasure but really had no overall purpose.

Through stepping back and analyzing what kind of more meaningful skills I had—and how I could help others through writing and spiritual studies—I am becoming more and more able to connect my creativity with my Higher Self.

Like many others with this placement of Saturn, I had to undergo some disappointments and bump up against dead ends before I found my correct pathway.

Snapshots of Romance, Saturn-Style

Here's one of the most dramatic, beautiful, joyous areas of life—romantic love. Well, for me, and others with Saturn in the Fifth House, there may be more drama, work, and intensity than sheer joy. Love carries with it complications and karmic lessons. It's the flip side of what we see and read in the commercials, advertisements, sitcoms, and romance novels. Those lucky folks with flirtatious, fortunate planets in the Fifth House (like Venus and Jupiter) will get asked out more often, will be more popular in general, and when love does come around there won't be as many issues as there are for those with a Fifth-House Saturn. It's the bumpy road to love, as the song goes.

Whether it's cheating hearts or objecting family members, love has always been challenging for me. I'll bet Romeo and/or Juliet had Saturn in the Fifth House.

Here's a snippet from my romantic history that might be illuminating for others like me.

In college, I was keeping a relationship with my high school boyfriend alive, and we found ourselves growing apart, which is normal. However, he did some rather mean things at times, like telling me about other women he was attracted to.

Any woman with high self-esteem would have just moved on. But I had such doubts about myself back then—about my desirability, my worth, my ability to attract friends of both sexes—that I stayed with him. Because folks with a Fifth-House Saturn lack "the flirtation gene," we often don't have as many possibilities for romantic partners as those around us. Other planets will, of course, weigh in on this. An affable Venus in the chart will counterbalance the coolness of Saturn in the Fifth, for example.

But for me, with the lack of emotional support and the demands of college, I figured it was better to hang on to a not-so-perfect romance than be alone. If only I'd had more courses in women's studies, I might have just told him it was time to split up.

What's ironic is that we ended up getting married. And there was a tacit understanding that I would just come home and pick up the routine where I had left off as a high school kid. I was worried about my own future and employability, and I preferred the company of my boyfriend to my conservative parents, so these desires for the structure marriage offered (Saturn rules structure) outweighed the little voice inside that wanted to break away from it all. Even if it wasn't a romantic twosome with powerful chemistry, I could be a pseudo-adult, living independently from my parents.

He was a good provider, we had a lot of history, and he could be a good friend, but he never seemed happy with me, especially my appearance. An intelligent, accomplished, well-read woman was okay as a wife, but not a romantic or sexual partner. Religion contributed to this mindset, as you can imagine—the old "good girl/bad girl" thing.

But good grief, I was young and beautiful. There were months and even years when we barely touched, which was never really addressed in a helpful, healing manner. Perhaps we just grew unexcited with each other, something counseling might have helped, but was left to sort itself out. Meanwhile, I truly thought I was unattractive and, sadly, not sexy. Again, Saturn in the Fifth House can cast doubts in an individual's mind about worthiness as far as love and romance go—which is ridiculous, if you think about it.

I was just married to the wrong guy, in a relationship without chemistry. It wasn't either person's fault; we had simply grown in different directions. This kind of heartache is very typical of Saturn in the house of love. The person knows love should feel different, but clings to the dysfunctional relationship, hoping that maybe, with work (Saturn), it can get better. Generally, there are delays, challenges, and issues about enjoying romance. Or, like I did, partners try therapy, read books, watch those family therapists on DVD. For me, there was no fixing this marriage, though, and it really fell apart not too long after my Saturn return.

Today, I'm married to an older, very kind, and talented man, and indeed, people with a Fifth-House Saturn often have relationships with older people, romantic and platonic. It hasn't been easy though. There were challenges from his grown children, financial obstacles, and even a generation gap. And I still get frustrated when he is attracted to some sweet young thing in a plunging neckline or a shiny, bright micro-mini skirt. (Maybe men are like fish, come to think of it—lured by shiny, bright things.) We work through these problems with the help of counseling. If we work hard enough, we'll get the hang of it, this time for sure. Now, that's Saturn for you. "With work, things will improve."

I acknowledge that I can have a detached, serious nature typical of Fifth-House Saturn. Like I said, we lack the flirtation gene.

Yet, I await the day when intelligence, honesty, wit, sensitivity, and kindness are the characteristics men look for in a woman, but I think I might be waiting forever in this sex- and youth-crazed culture. Maybe I belong in a country like France, where it is said that a woman doesn't become interesting until she turns forty.

Challenges with Children and Child-Rearing

Finally, there is the part of Fifth-House Saturn that many women are most troubled by. Because this is the house of children, and Saturn is the planet of restrictions, there have historically been issues with children and child-rearing associated with this placement. Saturn may delay the birth of children, which is not as troublesome as it used to be. Many women wait longer to have a family now and are helped along by the leaps and bounds in medicine and science, especially in vitro fertilization. I recently read about a woman who gave birth to twins at age fifty-five. (I think she must be nuts, personally.)

Or, there may be challenges surrounding motherhood—the child may need extra help because of mental or physical illness.

Or, when a person with a Fifth-House Saturn does have children, she could be a task-master, wanting her offspring to be like little adults, perhaps being overly critical or a strict disciplinarian.

Or, the person with a Fifth-House Saturn may bump into life challenges that put off child-bearing. For me, it was a frustrating first marriage, then years of shift work and un-stable relationships.

Fifth-House Saturn or not, in these times there are many, many women struggling with such problems—low pay, an erratic schedule, an absent partner. They can't support them-selves, so how are they supposed to raise children? Someone with a Fifth-House Saturn might work this out logically. But society tells us that it's unnatural to *not* have children—really hammers it home—so many women buy into this thinking and give birth to a little human who will live a life filled with neglect.

Some very young women have babies because it's "the thing to do" and then don't have a clue about raising them.

This, I guess, is my Saturnian practicality. I knew the timing for children wasn't right. I knew I couldn't be there for a child. When your own life is so complex, how can you find the focus to properly raise and love a child?

But for me, and others with Saturn in the Fifth House, it goes deeper.

Metaphorically, I had been "changing diapers" since I started dating, always waiting on people and taking care of them, cleaning up "their stuff." I knew enough about myself to believe that I deserved a time in my life—someday—that was just for me, where I could do the things I always wanted to do, live up to my potential, and perhaps help others realize theirs.

In a way, I knew this almost all my life. I don't know if this is yet another karmic thing—difficulties with children in a previous life, perhaps death from childbirth, perhaps over-whelmed by the number of children. Or perhaps I was reacting to my mom, who seemed to have so much potential and may have been grieving her lost opportunities.

Growing up as feminism caught fire, I considered my future, and there just didn't seem to be children in it. I have spoken to others with this same philosophy, including one client with a Fifth-House Saturn. Youngsters and babies just don't make this young lady as ex-cited as they would for women with different planetary placements.

She and I share this feeling that there are so many other things that resonate much more powerfully for us. For me, it's helping adults deal with psychological and spiritual growth, maybe even talking about deeper issues that have more to do with the end of life than the beginning.

This young lady also has dreams and passions that don't relate to bearing children. For one thing, she's a devoted student and has put her considerable energy and intelligence into studying law. Perhaps advocating for those who are less fortunate—helping to insti-tute societal and global change—interests her more than being home with little children. Plus, she's still quite young, so, true to Fifth-House Saturn, children might come later in life for her. (By the way, look to the Tenth House to see if there is a strong need for achieve-ment in the outer world as opposed to the home and hearth.)

Interestingly, this client is absolutely mad for animals and has a tender love for them that critters seem to recognize. When she came for a reading, my own cats wouldn't leave her alone. When they came in the room, I saw the most tender expression cross her face—unconditional love. See, she's not a hardhearted person just because she's not keen on children. Anyone who loves animals so much has a lot of heart-centered energy. In fact, if the Fifth House has challenges and the fourth chakra is blocked, gurus often suggest having an animal around to connect with the heart.

In short, there are many, many ways to be a "mother" or "parent" to the world or society. American culture, especially with this new traditionalism and conservatism coming into style, may look upon child-free women as cold and strange. If you have Saturn in this house, don't buy into this label or stereotype. You have to be true to yourself, act from the heart, and with a Fifth-House Saturn, the heart may beat loudly for many things aside from children. That's okay.

In addition (and this might sound shocking), many men might be happier if today's marriages didn't lead to children shortly after the vows are taken. When is a marriage about a partnership between two adults? When do adults get to rule the household, and not children? I look around and see that this is more and more the case—we exist for kids, and they seem to run everything.

Sometimes it's refreshing to be an adult in an adult world, especially for couples. Spoken like a true Fifth-House Saturn!

I laugh when I think about a recent situation that might fit those with a Fifth-House Saturn perfectly. I was having a massage in the back part of my chiropractor's office when suddenly a young child just started wailing and hollering and would not stop. I'm talking a future opera singer or rock star, with leather lungs and a piercing voice. This child would not be consoled.

I thought to myself, "Gad, that would drive me crazy. That's why I don't have children." Just at that moment, my masseuse (also child-free) said, "That's why I don't have children." We laughed.

Of course, watching and enjoying children and learning from their spontaneity outweighs an occasional temper tantrum. And sometimes I wonder if I am out of step with my fellow females. I know that motherhood is a kind of club where you are instantly welcomed. I also know that some women look down on child-free women, unfortunately.

I wish there was more openness about this issue. The groups Childfree by Choice and Population Connection (formerly Zero Population Growth) offer some food for thought to those who wish to pass on parenthood. Population Connection believes that being child-free an environmentally conscious decision, considering the population explosion, as well as future concerns like global warming and projections of a planetary shortage of natural resources, including water. So, not having children could contribute to the betterment of the planet, one person at a time. But our American culture is not ready for this kind of thinking. Consider the way even contraception is being challenged by some conservatives.

Bottom line, if you see Fifth-House Saturn in your chart and have always wanted children, then by all means go forth and be fruitful. But use the Saturnian wisdom to ask yourself the hard questions, such as "Will I be able to properly care for this child?" and "Is the timing right?" and "Would I be a nurturing parent, or do I have too many issues from my own childhood?" These questions can be answered with the help of a family therapist or counselor. An in-depth look at your astrological chart will also be helpful.

However, if family, friends, and the media are pressuring you to get out there and multiply and it's just not in your heart, stand up for your right to be child-free. Know there is a larger society out there where you can be a nurturer.

Use the Saturnian wisdom to raise your awareness, lighten up, and give love universally.

---

1. Caroline Myss, *Anatomy of the Spirit* (New York: Three Rivers Press, 1996).

Epilogue

I hope this trip through the various astrological houses has been entertaining and informative. It's been an education for me as well. Incidentally, for those who wish to understand where the planets are in their houses and need to get a complete natal horoscope, but don't know their birth times, I have a couple of suggestions.

You can sometimes, but not always, find it on your birth certificate.

Or, if your parents are still living, you can simply ask them or an older sibling. However, a sure-fire way to track down your birth time is to go to the source—the department of records at the hospital where you were born. Call the main switchboard and ask for this department, and sometimes you can give the records person your information directly. (Direct phone calls, I've learned, are more effective than e-mails.) They might need a few hours to get back to you. Or, they might suggest you write a formal request for this information and mail it to them, with a self-addressed, stamped envelope, so they can send it back to you. This takes a little longer, but has worked very well for me.

In addition, birth-record archives can sometimes be found in your county seat, or at the local branch of the National Archives, though this may require more legwork than you wish to do.

Once you have the time and place of birth, there are many resources to have a chart done. The Association for Research and Enlightenment in Virginia Beach, Virginia, provides astrology services through its bookshop. Before I got my own astrological software, this is where I sent all my queries. For more information, check its Web site, at http://www.edgarcayce.org. Llewellyn Publications also has a number of resources.

Or, contact your favorite astrologer. Astrologers may not be listed in the phone book, but you might see their services advertised in coffee shops or bookstores.

Good luck, and blessed be.

Selected Bibliography

Adler, Margot. *Drawing Down the Moon*. Boston: Beacon Press, 1986.

Allrich, Karri. *A Witch's Book of Dreams*. St. Paul, MN: Llewellyn Publications, 2001.

Avery, Jeanne. *Astrology and Your Health*. New York: Fireside Books, 1991.

Boldt, Laurence G. *Zen and the Art of Making a Living*. New York: Penguin, 1993.

Brady, Linda, and Evan St. Lifer. *Discovering Your Soul Mission*. New York: Three Rivers Press, 1998.

Burns, David D. *Feeling Good: The New Mood Therapy*. New York: Signet, 1981.

Callan, Dawn. *Awakening the Warrior Within*. Novato, CA: Nataraj Publications, 1995.

Camilleri, Stephanie. *The House Book*. St. Paul, MN: Llewellyn Publications, 1999.

Campbell, Joseph, with Bill Moyers. *The Power of Myth*. New York: Doubleday, 1988.

Cayce, Edgar. *My Life as a Seer: The Lost Memoirs*. Compiled and edited by A. Robert Smith. New York: St. Martin's Press, 1999.

Cerminara, Gina. *Many Mansions*. 1950. Reprint, New York: Morrow, 1968.

Devlin, Mary. *Astrology and Past Lives*. West Chester, PA: Para Research/Schiffer Publishing, 1987.

Dreher, Diane. *The Tao of Inner Peace*. New York: Harper Perennial, 1991.

———. *The Tao of Womanhood*. New York: Quill/William Morrow, 1998.

Elysian Group. "Astro House Systems," *Elysian Astrology & New Age Shop*. Article available online at http://www.elysian.co.uk/astrologyhousesystems.htm (accessed March 2006).

Gawain, Shakti. *Creative Visualization*. New York: Bantam, 1982.

Gibson, Lindsay. *Who You Were Meant to Be*. Far Hills, NJ: New Horizon Press, 2000.

Golomb, Elan. *Trapped in the Mirror*. New York: William Morrow, 1992.

Gross, Philippe L., and S. I. Shapiro. *The Tao of Photography*. Berkeley, CA: Ten Speed Press, 2001.

Hay, Louise. *You Can Heal Your Life*. Carlsbad, CA: Hay House, 2004.

Hickey, Isabel M. *Astrology: A Cosmic Science*. Sebastopol, CA: CRCS Publications, 1982.

Huxley, Aldous. *Brave New World*. New York: Harper and Brothers, 1932.

Jung, Carl Gustav. *The Basic Writings of C. G. Jung*. New York: The Modern Library, 1959.

Kempton-Smith, Debbi. *Secrets from a Stargazer's Notebook*. New York: Topquark Press, 1999.

Koolman, Margaret. *Soul Purpose Astrology*. St. Paul: Llewellyn Publications, 2002.

Kübler-Ross, Elisabeth. *Death Is of Vital Importance*. Barrytown, NY: Station Hill Press, 1995.

Lane, Barbara. *16 Clues to Your Past Lives!* Virginia Beach, VA: A.R.E. Press, 1999.

Leary, Timothy, with R. U. Sirius. *Design for Dying*. San Francisco: HarperEdge, 1997.

Lofthus, Myrna. *A Spiritual Approach to Astrology*. Sebastopol, CA: CRCS Publications, 1983.

McGraw, Phillip C. *Life Strategies*. New York: Hyperion, 1999.

Myss, Caroline. *Anatomy of the Spirit*. New York: Three Rivers Press, 1996.

Noble, Vicki. *Motherpeace: A Way to the Goddess Through Myth, Art, and Tarot*. San Francisco: Harper & Row, 1983.

Parker, Julia and Derek. *K.I.S.S. Guide to Astrology*. London: Dorling Kindersley, 2000.

River, Lindsay, and Sally Gillespie. *The Knot of Time*. New York: Harper & Row, 1987.

Rodden, Lois. *Lois Rodden's AstroDatabank* Web site, http://www.astrodatabank.com.

Simpson, Dr. Shepherd. "Development of House Systems after Classical Astrology." Article available online at http://www.geocities.com/astrologyhouses/housesystems.htm (accessed March 2006).

Todeschi, Kevin. *Soul Development: Edgar Cayce's Approach for a New World*. Virginia Beach, VA: A.R.E. Press, 2003.

White, Ruth. *Karma & Reincarnation*. York Beach, ME: Samuel Weiser, 1987.

Williamson, Marianne. *A Return to Love: Reflections on the Principles of A Course in Miracles*. New York: Harper Collins, 1992.

Zukav, Gary. *The Seat of the Soul*. New York: Fireside, 1990.